PRAY & SING

Prayers & Songs in the New Testament

Doug Rowston

Praying and singing went together for followers of Jesus in the first century. The New Testament includes fine examples of profound prayers and sacred songs. This book opens the pages of the New Testament and looks at nine prayers, seven songs and an eighth set of songs to God and Christ in the power of the Spirit.

The examination of these prayers and songs will encourage twenty-first century seekers after truth to pray to the Lord and to sing his praises. Indeed, taking seriously the New Testament prayers and songs will enable readers to be followers of Jesus who practise what they preach.

Rowston, Doug
PRAY & SING: Prayers & Songs in the New Testament

Published by
Grace & Peace Books
4A Wurilba Ave Hawthorn SA 5062 Australia
djrowston@gmail.com

© Douglas James Rowston 2011

This work is copyright. All photographs were taken by the author. Other than for the purposes and subject to the conditions prescribed under the Copyright Act, no part of it may in any form or by any means (electronic, mechanical, microcopying, photocopying, recording or otherwise) be reproduced, stored in a retrieval system or transmitted without prior written permission from the publisher.

First published 2012 by MediaCom Education Inc
This edition published in 2022

ISBN 978-0-6453288-2-0

1. Bible. N.T. - Prayers.
2. Bible. N.T. - Hymns

248.32

Acknowledgements

Bible quotations are from the New Revised Standard Version Bible, Anglicized Edition, copyright © 1989, 1995 by the Division of Christian Education of the National Council of Churches of Christ in the U S A. Used by permission. All rights reserved.

Cover photographs
Front: Queensland sunrise
Back: Canadian sunset

*This book is dedicated
to Colin and Sarah
my son and daughter
who were very young
when their mother died.
She would be proud of
what they have done
in the succeeding years
and who they have become.*

Contents

Introduction   1

PRAY

1	The Model Prayer	5
2	The Father and the Son	23
3	The Testament of Jesus	29
4	The Theology of Prayer	37
5	The Prayer of the Trinity	41
6	The Testament of Paul	45
7	The God of Peace	51
8	The God of Grace and Glory	55
9	The Presence of God	59

SING

10	The Saviour	65
11	The Prophet of the Most High	71
12	The Master	77
13	The Word	81
14	The Mind of Christ	91
15	The Firstborn	97
16	The Son	103
17	The Lord and the Lamb	109

Postscript   121
Select Bibliography   125

Dr Doug Rowston lives in Adelaide, South Australia, with his wife Rosalie and their noble canine a Welsh Corgi dog. He is a Baptist Minister who has worked as theological lecturer at Burleigh College, religious education teacher at Prince Alfred College, pastor of Richmond Baptist Church, and adjunct lecturer at St Barnabas College (Charles Sturt University).

Doug has also written *A Bird's Eye View of the Bible (Second Edition); Jesus and Life: Word Pictures in John's Gospel; Promises & Blessings in the Book of Revelation; Things that Jesus said: Parables of the Kingdom & Eternal Life; Things that Jesus did: Miracles of the Kingdom & Signs of Eternal Life; From Unread to Misread: Hebrews to Revelation Neglected New Testament Books.*

Introduction

At times we may find it hard to pray. Personal and public prayers can be a mixture of written prayers, prayers with or without notes, on the spur of the moment prayers. They can be as basic as 'Thank you, Lord!' and 'Help us, Lord!' or as intricate as the General Confession and the General Thanksgiving. As we read the Bible and meditate upon its message this can move us into prayer of different kinds.

Paul urges us to *pray without ceasing (1 Thessalonians 5:17)* and to *persevere in prayer (Romans 12:12)*. This is probably because it's a valuable way of relating to God in every aspect of life. As James Montgomery wrote, 'Prayer is the soul's sincere desire, uttered or unexpressed.'

Prayer can include:
praising God for his creating, preserving, saving presence,
confessing our sins to God,
thanking God for his good gifts in life and faith,
asking God for general and specific requests,
giving to God what we are and what we have to his service.

With good reason Christians usually offer these different kinds of prayer to God through Jesus the Lord and Saviour. He prayed and he taught his disciples to pray. As we shall see, his followers prayed and set a fine example of how to pray in the pages of the New Testament.

Some of us may also admit that we find it hard to sing ... in tune! I certainly enjoy singing traditional hymns and praise songs in unison at church. However, please do not ask me to sing in a group with different parts! Our musical tastes can be many and varied, sacred and secular, instrumental and vocal.

Paul also encourages us to *sing psalms, hymns, and spiritual songs to God (Colossians 3:16)* and to *be filled with the Spirit, as you sing psalms and hymns and spiritual songs among yourselves (Ephesians 5:18b-19a)*.

The Bible's sacred songs include the Psalms in the Old Testament. The New Testament also has sacred songs. Luke's narrative about the young church mentions an incident at Philippi involving two jailed believers. *About midnight Paul and Silas were praying and singing hymns to God, and the prisoners were listening to them.(Acts 16:25)* Praying and singing went together for followers of Jesus.

In the early second century the governor of Pontus and Bithynia (in northern Turkey today) wrote a letter to the emperor in Rome. Pliny asked Trajan about certain believers who 'were in the habit of meeting before dawn on a stated day and singing alternately a hymn to Christ as to a god'.

Pliny told Trajan that these Christians took an oath not to commit sins or crimes and held a common meal. Singing sacred songs to God through Christ, commitment to a new lifestyle, and sharing a common meal in memory of Christ had parallels in the worship of the earliest believers.

According to Luke, believers met regularly in homes and *devoted themselves to the apostles' teaching and fellowship, to the breaking of bread and the prayers.(Acts 2:42)*

Their worship consisted of the apostles' teaching, the offering of gifts to help the needy, the breaking of bread and drinking of wine to remember the Lord until he comes, and the offering of prayer to praise, confess, thank, ask, and surrender to God.

Against this background the first section of the book seeks to deepen our understanding of prayers in the New Testament.

We begin with the Lord's Prayer. I call it the Model Prayer. It covers God's glory and human needs. Of course, it was given to us by Jesus, in whom God comes to us and through whom we go to God. We look at two other prayers of Jesus as well. Then we examine Paul's theology of prayer in his finest letter before discussing two more prayers of the apostle. The last selected prayers come from Hebrews, First Peter, and Jude.

When we turn to consider some songs in the New Testament, we meet a wealth of elevated language and deep devotion to God through Christ. The elevated language includes the use of parallelism. Modern English translations of the New Testament sometimes reproduce this linguistic feature in poetry. The deep devotion to God through Christ apparently took place in early Christian worship.

In this context the second section of the book seeks to deepen our appreciation of songs in the New Testament. Of course, these songs were sung prayerfully by believers.

We commence with three songs in Luke's record of the births of John the Baptist and Jesus of Nazareth. Then we negotiate the heights and depths of the song at the beginning of John's Gospel. After this we look at two songs in Paul's letters to the Christians at Philippi and Colossae. Next we examine a truly memorable song at the beginning of Hebrews. Finally, we discuss songs in Revelation about the Lord and the Lamb.

The examination of these prayers and songs will encourage twenty-first century seekers after truth to pray to the Lord and to sing his praises. Indeed, taking seriously the New Testament prayers and songs will enable us all to be followers of Jesus who live the Christian life.

1 The Model Prayer

Rowan Williams, former Archbishop of Canterbury, has remarked, 'If somebody said, "Give me a summary of Christian faith on the back of an envelope," the best thing to do would be to write the Lord's Prayer.'

Our Father in heaven, hallowed be your name, your kingdom come, your will be done, on earth as it is in heaven. Give us this day our daily bread. And forgive us our debts, as we also have forgiven our debtors. And do not bring us to the time of trial, but rescue us from the evil one.(Matthew 6:9-13)

Introduction

At the lowest level, prayer is shouting into a seemingly empty space in hope that someone somewhere is listening. I recall a visit to a Buddhist temple near Dehra Dun in Northern India. I watched an old woman walking around the perimeter, twirling a hand held prayer clacker, pushing big prayer cylinders, and seeking to gain merit. To me this was prayer at the lowest level.

At the highest level, prayer is sensing the presence of God becoming so real that we are lifted up to face the joys and sorrows of life. As Paul said, *Likewise the Spirit helps us in our weakness; for we do not know how to pray as we ought, but that very Spirit intercedes with sighs too deep for words. (Romans 8:26)* Prayer is God's abiding presence made real.

Prayer was so important to Jesus that he taught his disciples to pray. Jesus told his followers to pray without empty phrases and in not many words. *When you are praying, do not heap up empty phrases as the Gentiles do; for they think that they will be heard because of their many words. Do not be like them, for your Father knows what you need before you ask him.(Matthew 6:7-8)*

We are to beware of *empty phrases*. In the original Greek the word imitates the sound associated with the thing designated. A good translation would be 'babble'. We are to beware of *many words*. We may have encountered people who think that they will be heard for their much speaking. Quality wins over quantity in conversations between humans and in conversations with God.

There are two versions of the Lord's Prayer, one in Matthew 6:9-13 and the other in Luke 11:2-4. The basic content of both versions goes back to Jesus. Matthew's version may be addressed to people who have learned to pray long ago but are in danger of praying routinely. Luke's version may be addressed to people who are just learning to pray but are in need of courage to pray.

Matthew's version is longer and probably has been elaborated in a Jewish Christian church. Luke's version is shorter and probably has been handed down in a Gentile Christian community of faith.

Our Father in heaven

Jesus teaches us to address God as *Our Father* and allows us as his disciples to be related to the Creator of all things great and small. We have the privilege of relating to God's might, majesty, and power in the role of a child of God.

If we stand on the edge of something like the Grand Canyon and look down into its gaping chasm, we sense the awesome power of creation and preservation. If we visit a large European church and hear the majestic tones of a pipe organ reaching every nook and cranny, we also sense the elusive presence of something or someone beyond us.

People can speak vaguely, or even flippantly, of such a power and a presence as the Great Spirit, the Man Upstairs, the First Cause, the Ground of Being, the Supreme Mystery, the Ultimate Concern, or the Great Someone in the Great Somewhere.

Jesus helps us to speak personally of Our Father. The heavenly Father is the God of Jesus. He is creating, preserving, rescuing, and restoring people like us, people who are made in his image, people for whom Christ died and rose again.

Joachim Jeremias, the knowledgeable and humble German scholar, examined *The Central Message of the New Testament* in four lectures. The first lecture entitled 'Abba' is relevant to our understanding of the model prayer. In the time of Jesus it would have been unthinkable to call God by the Aramaic word *Abba* which lies behind the Greek word for Father. There is proof that Jesus used this word in a daringly new way (Mark

14:36). He spoke to God in prayer as a child to its father confidently and securely, reverently and obediently.

Jeremias goes so far as to say that Jesus was aware of a unique revelation in that God reveals himself to Jesus as only a father can reveal himself to a son. So Jesus is the man for others, the man who has the power to address God as Father and the man who has the authority to allow sinners like us to call God *Our Father in heaven.*

Note the balance: near and far, intimacy and reverence. Jesus knew God as Father, near and intimate, and Jesus recognised God as in heaven, far and reverent.

The followers of Jesus believe that God is near but they are not pantheists, who believe that God is everything and everything is God. The followers of Jesus believe that God is far but they are not deists, who believe that God is distant and out of reach. The followers of Jesus believe that God is revealed in Jesus but they are not sentimentalists, who treat God as a benevolent grandfather.

When our words are too informal, we are nevertheless taken into the presence of the mighty God who has the whole world in his hands. When our words are too formal, we are nevertheless met in the midst of life by the merciful God who suffers on the old rugged cross.

According to Rowan Williams, when we join Jesus in praying, *Our Father in heaven,* Jesus is saying to us, '*The relationship I have with God can be your relationship with God as well. You and I form a We together before God.*'

Hallowed be your name

Shakespeare penned these words in *Romeo and Juliet*:
What's in a name? that which we call a rose
By any other name would smell as sweet.

What's in a name if it's God's name? An aweful (not awful) lot, if you are Moses in the Old Testament. Moses is the person to whom God revealed his special name. In revealing his name, God is revealing his nature. The God of Moses is not like the gods of Egypt that are in material form such as Amun, the god of the Pharaoh, Anubis, the god of the cemeteries, Horus, the god of the sky, Isis, the mother goddess, Osiris, the fertility god, and Re, the sun god. The God of Moses cannot be represented by such images. God can only be represented by his name.

And what is the name of God? In the book of Exodus God tells Moses to say, *'I AM WHO I AM (*or *I WILL BE WHAT I WILL BE). . . I AM has sent me to you.' (Exodus 3:14)* God also tells Moses to say, *'The LORD (*or *YHWH), the God of your ancestors, the God of Abraham, the God of Isaac, and the God of Jacob, has sent me to you.' (Exodus 3:15)*

The noun *'YHWH'* in Exodus 3:15 is related to the verb *'I AM'* in Exodus 3:14. The usual translation *'I AM WHO I AM'* points towards God's eternal being. God is always there. The other translation *'I WILL BE WHAT I WILL BE'* points to God's active presence in history. God causes things to happen.

The Old Testament story inseparably holds together the Name, *YHWH*, and the Saving Will of God. No wonder that the name of God was kept holy in Old Testament times. Indeed, the Jewish people came to say *Adonai* (Lord) instead of Yahweh (the likely pronunciation of *YHWH*) out of reverence for the Divine Name.

What's in a name if it's God's name? An aweful lot, if you are Jesus in the New Testament. Jesus tells us to pray, *Hallowed be your name. (Matthew 6:9)* Hallowed does not mean Harold, the name of a Colorado friend, Harrold, my wife Rosalie's maiden name, or Hello, the Australian equivalent of the American Hi, or The Herald, the former evening newspaper in Melbourne!

Hallowed means to be kept holy, to be honoured. The name is God's Name, indicating his nature and being. Jesus is probably drawing on the prayer prayed at the end of synagogue services, 'Hallowed be his great name in the world, and may his kingdom come in your lifetime and in your days.'

Martin Luther in his catechism asked, 'How is God's name hallowed amongst us?' Luther then answered the question quite memorably, 'When both our life and doctrine are truly Christian.'

Holiness is what God is and is what God wants to give. No wonder the New Testament tells Christians to be holy in all their behaviour because God is holy (1 Peter 1:15).

So, what's in a name if it's the name of God? A lot of awe. When we're talking about God we are acknowledging that we serve the Source, Guide, and Goal of all that is. Believe it or not, God is our Father.

Your kingdom come

We live in a world looking for the next big thing. When will a drought break? When will wars end? When will there be peace between Israelis and Palestinians? When will the second coming take place? Even Christians who have prayed *Your kingdom come* have tried to set dates for the next big thing.

For example, a Baptist named William Miller, ordained in 1833, published lectures on the second coming in 1835. As a Bible student he had pondered the Book of Daniel and interpreted its reference to 2300 days (Daniel 8:14) as 2300 years and had concluded that the end of the world would come on March 21, 1843. When it didn't, he recalculated the date of the end as March 21, 1844.

When it still didn't come, a fellow believer named Samuel Snow made another recalculation, October 22, 1844. Out of the 'great disappointment' came a reinterpretation and the birth of the Seventh Day Adventist movement. Miller, in the mean time, died a sick, discouraged, and abandoned figure who presided over a small Vermont Adventist congregation in his last days. Of course, Miller is not the only person to set dates for the second coming. The names of David Koresh and Hal Lindsey come to mind in recent years.

When is God's kingdom, the royal reign of God, coming? As we pray the model prayer, we discover that the kingdom has begun to come and the kingdom is still to come.

There is an old hymn which says, in non-inclusive language:
>   Rise up O men of God,
>   Have done with lesser things;
>   Give heart and soul and mind and strength
>   To serve the King of kings.

There is also a parody of it which reads:
>   Sit down O men of God,
>   His Kingdom he will bring,
>   Just as and when and where he will,
>   You cannot do a thing.

The contrast is falsely drawn. The kingdom of heaven is both active and passive, both present and future. Human beings are to be fully committed and involved. This is through the strength and purpose which God supplies. The kingdom is being actualised in the first coming of Jesus and in the work of his followers, but it will only be consummated at the final coming of Jesus.

Your will be done

When bad things happen to a good person, people sometimes say that it is the will of God. But it isn't necessarily so. We may differentiate meanings of 'the will of God'.

There is the **intentional** will of God. This is the ideal plan of God for all people. When we see the glory of the Lord reflected on this good earth in moral, healthy, happy people, we know that this is what God intends. There is also the **circumstantial** will of God. That is the plan of God for certain circumstances. When we see the grace of the Lord present in the sufferer of some horrible disease, we know that this is the right reaction to the wrong situation. The reaction, not the situation, is the will of God. There is finally the **ultimate** will of God, the full and final realisation of God's purpose in spite of circumstances.

When I was in year 11 at school, I had to read Thomas Hardy's novel, *The Mayor of Casterbridge*. I can't remember much about the book. Hardy also wrote other novels including *Tess of the d'Urbervilles* in 1891, which attracted criticism for its sympathetic portrayal of a 'fallen woman'. It was subtitled, *A Pure Woman: Faithfully Narrated*. The agnostic Hardy finished this book with the words, 'The President of the Immortals had ended his sport with Tess.'

But we do not believe in a god who plays sport with human lives. We do believe in the God who made us to create what is beautiful, to believe what is true, to do what is right. We do believe in the God who so loved us that he gave his unique Son to rescue and restore us by faith through grace. It is right and proper for us to pray for the fulfilment of what God has willed: the beautiful, the true, and the right.

On earth as it is in heaven

Hallowed be your name is about the holiness of God's name. *Your kingdom come* puts a face on the name and requests the overthrow of evil and death. *Your will be done* celebrates the reign of goodness and life. All of this is to be *On earth as it is in heaven*. We are praying for the union of heaven and earth.

As Tom Wright reminds us, hallowing the name, the kingdom coming, and doing the will of God is like the cure of a dreadful disease and the performance of a musical masterpiece. Jesus is like a medical genius who discovers a remarkable medicine. The followers of Jesus are like doctors, being cured by the medicine and applying it to those who need it. Jesus is like a musical genius who writes a wonderful piece of music. The followers of Jesus are like musicians, entranced by the music and performing it before a world full of discord.

The name of God, the kingdom of heaven, and the will of God have come in the person and work of Jesus. As Jesus said, *The time is fulfilled, and the kingdom of God has come near; repent, and believe in the good news. (Mark 1:15)*

The name of God, the kingdom of heaven, and the will of God are yet to come in their fullness at the final coming of Jesus. As Jesus promised, *And this good news of the kingdom will be proclaimed throughout the world, as a testimony to all the nations; and then the end will come.(Matthew 24:14)*

In the meantime, we are being cured by God's medicine in Christ and applying it to others. In the meantime, we are being entranced by God's music in Christ and performing it for others.

Give us this day our daily bread

In the model prayer Jesus teaches us that God wants us to share what's on our mind, to be part of a conversation, and to draw closer to him. God knows that we have needs and so we say, 'Give us', not 'Give me'. Christianity is not only an individual commitment, it is also a communal commitment.

We also say, 'Give us this day', not 'Give us next year'. Christianity is a day by day experience. We do not know what the future will bring. We do know who goes into the future with us.

Finally, we say, 'Give us this day our daily bread.' This is a request for bread, the staple diet of the ordinary person in the time of Jesus. There is one puzzling word in this part of the model prayer. It can be translated 'daily' or 'for tomorrow'.

If the meaning is 'daily bread', as in the text of the major translations, it is suitable for a morning prayer regarding the day just begun. We recall the story of the wilderness journey of the Israelites out of Egypt under the leadership of Moses in Exodus 16. God was going to rain down *bread from heaven* for the people. All they had to do in the morning was to gather enough for each day. When they saw the *fine flaky substance* on the ground, they said, *"What is it?"* (Hebrew, *man hu*) This *manna* is what the Israelites ate during their wanderings until they came to the promised land. It was their daily bread.

If the meaning is 'bread for tomorrow', as in the margin of modern translations of the Bible, it is appropriate for an evening prayer with a view to the next morning meal before going to work. We think of a hard working farmer, a persistent fisher, or a conscientious carpenter. Such a worker has a daily dependence on God for life's necessities.

We pray 'Give us this day our daily bread', not 'Give us this day our daily cake'. Marie Antoinette (1755-1793) was the Austrian princess who married King Louis XVI of France. His coronation took place at Reims during the height of a bread shortage in Paris. This is the context in which Marie Antoinette is quoted as joking, 'If they have no bread, then let them eat cake!' Jesus teaches us to pray for what we need, bread, rather than what we want, cake.

When our prayer for daily bread has been answered we can express our thankfulness. Ben Witherington tells the story of a Christian farmer who was spending the day in a nearby large city. Entering a restaurant at noon, he found a table near a group of young men. When his meal was served, he quietly bowed his head and gave thanks for the food before him. Observing this, the young men thought they would ridicule and embarrass the man. One called out in a loud voice, 'Hey hillbilly, does everyone do that where you live?' Looking the rude youth straight in the face, the old man said calmly: 'No, son, the pigs don't.'

Forgive us our debts

Jesus deals with things differently to the world in which we live. Our world imagines, or denies, or lives with guilt for sins, but does not deal with real guilt for real sins. Overall, we are inclined to commit sins but we find it hard to admit that we do so.

The early church listed seven deadly sins: idolatry, blasphemy, murder, adultery, fornication, false witness, and fraud. The medieval church produced another list of seven mortal sins: pride, covetousness, lust, anger, gluttony, envy, and sloth.

One of the best ways of describing sins is found in the General Confession from the Anglican Prayer Book: *Almighty and most merciful Father, we have strayed from your ways like lost sheep, we have followed too much the devices and desires of our own hearts, we have offended against your holy laws. We have left undone what we ought to have done, and we have done what we ought not to have done.*

The New Testament has three words for sin.

In Matthew 6:12 the word ***debts*** indicates a sense of moral obligation which we have to God and others. When we fail to meet our obligations, we owe debts.

In Matthew 6:14-15 the word ***trespasses*** pictures a set of reasonable boundaries which mark our relationship with God and others. When we overstep the boundaries, we commit trespasses.

In Luke 11:4 the word ***sins*** signifies instances of missing the target of life by failing to keep religious and moral laws. When we miss the mark, we do wrong and are guilty of sinful offences.

As we also have forgiven our debtors

Whatever word is used for sin, the model prayer encourages us to seek forgiveness and that involves the restoration of relationships. Forgiveness received by us is linked with forgiveness offered to others. If we are not forgiving, we place an impediment in our own lives and prevent the reception of divine forgiveness.

As Jesus says, *For if you forgive others their trespasses, your heavenly Father will also forgive you; but if you do not forgive others, neither will your Father forgive your trespasses.*

(Matthew 6:14-15) What blocks the flow of forgiveness from us blocks the flow of forgiveness to us.

Jesus himself practised what he preached when he prayed on the cross, *"Father, forgive them; for they do not know what they are doing."(Luke 23:34)* Jesus set the example for us to follow in forgiving others who have wronged us. He even forgave his enemies.

Jesus tells a parable about an unmerciful servant in Matthew 18:21-35. A man owes a king a fortune. Even so, the king forgives the man. However, the forgiven debtor is owed a pittance by a fellow servant. The man who has been forgiven an astronomical amount seizes his debtor by the throat and throws him into the debtors' prison. All is not lost. Fellow servants are extremely upset and report the matter to the king. The king who had previously been merciful is now very angry. The servant is now unforgiven, again in debt, and he is at the mercy of the torturers. He now knows the truth of the words, 'Don't forgive - and see what happens!'

It's a parable about God the Judge. On the one hand, where God's forgiveness produces a readiness to forgive, there God's mercy grants forgiveness of the sins of the forgiver. On the other hand, where the unforgiving servant abuses God's gift, there God's judgement dispenses severity upon the unforgiving, as if he had never been forgiven by God.

Jesus encourages us to pray: 'Our heavenly Father, forgive us our sins, just as we on a lesser scale forgive those who sin against us.' An unforgiving Christian is a contradiction. How can we appreciate God's forgiveness if we don't forgive our fellow human? If we persist in unforgiveness, we can end up like the unmerciful servant who forfeited his initial forgiveness due to his hard hearted unforgiving ways.

Years ago somebody did something which hurt someone very much. Time passed and both moved on. The victim was attending an interstate conference. During a break he was reading a book for review in a journal. It was on the Lord's Prayer! He was going all right until he reached the words, *And forgive us our debts, as we also have forgiven our debtors.* Fortunately, another person was at the conference who understood his dilemma. He wrote a letter of forgiveness, checked it out with his trusted friend, and sent it to the person who had wronged him. He felt that a load had been lifted off his shoulders. He had been letting his unforgiving attitude poison his life.

Forgiveness is like teaching a child to do something. The mother or father does it carefully a few times. Then the parent steps back and says, 'Now you show me how to do it.' God has forgiven us and has stepped back. He is saying to us, 'Now you show me how to forgive.'

Do not bring us to the time of trial

Again Jesus deals with things differently to the world in which we live. Our world minimises evil, or wallows in evil, or fights zealously against evil. But our world does not confront evil with Jesus and the victory of God. Overall, we tend to yield to temptations but find it easy to blame something or someone else. We remember the comedian who was always saying, 'The devil made me do it!'

Do not bring means 'Don't allow us to be brought.' According to James, *Whenever you face trials of any kind, consider it nothing but joy, because you know that the testing of your faith produces endurance ... No one, when tempted, should say,"I am being tempted by God"; for God ... tempts no one. But one is tempted by one's own desire ... (James 1:2-3, 13-14)*

There is a Jewish prayer which reads, 'Lead me not into the power of transgression. And bring me not into the power of sin, and not into the power of iniquity, and not into the power of temptation, and not into the power of anything shameful.'

The time of trial can mean 'an extreme test'. Jesus in Gethsemane says, *Pray that you may not come into the time of trial.(Matthew 26:41) The time of trial* can also mean 'the last great trial'. John on Patmos mentions *the hour of trial that is coming on the whole world to test the inhabitants of the earth. (Revelation 3:10)* Yes, *the time of trial* can mean a combination of both 'an extreme test' and 'the last great trial'. Jesus foretold times of persecution and promised his followers, *But the one who endures to the end will be saved.(Matthew 24:13)*

Rescue us from the evil one

Rescue us from evil refers to rescue from the evil, that is, the power of evil, or the principle of evil. An early Christian document says, 'Remember, Lord, your Church, to save it from **all** evil.' (Didache 10:5) It is worth noting that ordinary testings and temptations are manifestations of the ultimate power of evil. We are to see them as threats to faith and faithfulness and we are to ask for God's deliverance from them.

The ideas of temptation and preservation go together. For example, one scholar translates the section: 'Put us not to the test, rather deliver us from the Evil One.' Another scholar sharpens the meaning of the words and suggests, 'Let us not succumb to the trial, that is to say, O Lord, preserve us from falling away, but deliver us from evil.'

The negative of temptation is being balanced by the positive of preservation: *And do not bring us to the time of trial, but rescue us from the evil one.*

According to Tom Long, this is a way of saying, 'Keep us safe out there, O God. Let the forces of evil tremble to see us coming, rather than the other way around, and bring us home at the end of this day even stronger in faith than when we go out.'

The traditional version of the model prayer concludes with a doxology. *For the kingdom and the power and the glory are yours for ever. Amen.* These words appear in the margin of modern translations of the Bible because they were not in the original text of Matthew's Gospel. When the Lord's Prayer began to be used by early Christians in worship, they added words of praise based on King Solomon's prayer in 1 Chronicles 29:11-12.

Conclusion

As we pray the model prayer of Jesus, commonly called the Lord's Prayer, we do three things:
    We open ourselves to God in trust and praise.
    We receive his gifts freely.
    We yield to his demands willingly.

It was Jesus who called God Father, who honoured God's name, who realised the coming of God's kingdom, and who did God's will on earth as in heaven.

It was Jesus who fed the hungry, who offered forgiveness to the repentant, who himself passed the great trial, and who delivered us once and for all from the power of death and evil.

Jesus tells us to use imperatives throughout the model prayer: let your name be honoured, let your kingdom come, let your will be done, give us our daily bread, do not bring us to trial, rescue us from evil. These commands record the fact of the acts.

We pray for the Heavenly Father's glory: the honouring of God's name, the coming of God's rule, the doing of God's will.

We pray for the meeting of humanity's needs: provision of food, pardon for sins, protection from evil.

The model prayer is indeed a summary of Christian faith.

2 Father and Son

Jesus is aware of his mission to reveal his Father. God has given him the revelation of himself as much as only a father can reveal himself to his son. Jesus alone is able to pass on to others the real knowledge and understanding of God. Jesus, who has received the revelation of God, is able to mediate the knowledge of God.

Introduction

At the end of Matthew 11, in the midst of various responses to his mission and message, Jesus highlights the importance of childlike trust for the true citizens of the kingdom of heaven.

Prayer of the Son to the Father

I thank you, Father, Lord of heaven and earth, because you have hidden these things from the wise and the intelligent and have revealed them to infants; yes, Father, for such was your gracious will.(Matthew 11:25-26)

Jesus the Son gives thanks to God the Father. The people of childlike trust, not the so called wise and intelligent, have received the revelation of the kingdom of heaven. Revelation is personal. It involves trusting, knowing, loving, and serving Jesus who is the kingdom in himself. As John's Gospel puts it, *And this is eternal life, that they may know you, the only true God, and Jesus Christ whom you have sent. (John 17:3)*

Revelation is also powerful, as Jesus gives us, in Paul Tillich's phrase, 'The Courage To Be'.

Meditation on the Father and the Son

All things have been handed over to me by my Father; and no one knows the Son except the Father, and no one knows the Father except the Son and anyone to whom the Son chooses to reveal him.(Matthew 11:27)

A nineteenth century German scholar, Karl von Hase, the great grandfather of Dietrich Bonhoeffer, said that this saying 'gives the impression of a thunderbolt fallen from the Johannine sky'. The two features which supposedly pointed in this direction were the idea of mutual knowledge and the designation of Jesus as 'the Son'. However, it can be argued that the implicit saying in Matthew 11:27//Luke 10:22 based on Aramaic could have influenced the explicit statements in John expressed in Greek.

For example, John's Gospel opens with the thought that the community of faith had seen the glory of Christ, *the glory as of the Father's only Son, full of grace and truth.(John 1:14c)* John's Gospel also includes the saying of Jesus, *Very truly, I tell you, the Son can do nothing on his own, but only what he sees the Father doing; for whatever the Father does, the Son does likewise.(John 5:19)* The first three Gospels are probably closer to the actual words of Jesus in Aramaic but the fourth Gospel still conveys the actual voice of Jesus in Greek.

The first line of the meditation on the Father and the Son, *All things have been handed over to me by my Father*, introduces the theme: 'My Father has given me a full revelation.' The next two lines, *and no one knows the Son except the Father, and no one knows the Father except the Son*, elaborate the relationship between the Son and the Father. The fourth line, *and anyone to whom the Son chooses to reveal him*, suggests that the Son alone is in the position to pass on the knowledge of the Father to others.

Invitation to the weary and burdened

Come to me, all you that are weary and are carrying heavy burdens, and I will give you rest. Take my yoke upon you, and learn from me; for I am gentle and humble in heart, and you will find rest for your souls. For my yoke is easy, and my burden is light.(Matthew 11:28-30)

We are to come not to the modern equivalents of ancient gods such as Mars (War), Mammon (Money), Aphrodite (Sex), Gaia (Mother Nature), Polytheism (Pluralism), Bacchus and the Corn Gods (Drink and Food), Mantras and Mysticism (Inward Illumination), Idols of the Mind (Rationalism).

We are to come to the true God of every age. Perhaps we are weary trying to keep up with the Joneses, or seeking satisfaction in all the wrong places, or hoping to win a huge lottery, or trying to earn our salvation without God's help. Jesus promises to give us refreshment and renewal.

In terms of Paul Tillich's analysis, Jesus empowers us to overcome the anxieties of fate and death, guilt and condemnation, emptiness and meaninglessness. Jesus does this as we experience the power of the Resurrection, the forgiveness of the Cross, and the purpose of the Spirit.

Jesus tells us to take his yoke upon us. A yoke joins a pair of draught animals, especially oxen. It consists of a crosspiece with two bow shaped pieces underneath, one at each end, with each bow enclosing the head of the animal. In the time of Jesus farmers would use wooden yokes to guide oxen. The oxen were measured, the yoke was made, the yoke was put on the oxen, and the yoke was adjusted to fit the oxen's necks comfortably.

The Jewish rabbis spoke of the yoke of the law as a symbol of obedience to the wise instruction of God. Jesus also speaks of the yoke as a symbol of obedience to God's commandments, loving God and loving our neighbour. A yoke was made for two. Jesus never imposes upon his follower a yoke which he himself does not also bear.

Jesus says that his yoke is *easy*, well fitted and not harsh, easy to wear, and his burden is *light*, shared and not heavy, easy to bear, because *rest* is given by the *gentle* and *humble* one. Jesus shares our weakness, is devoted to the Father, and brings us into unity with God's will.

As we know, Jesus was a carpenter (Mark 6:3), and his earthly father, Joseph, was also a carpenter (Matthew 13:55). William Barclay, with some poetic licence, suggests that there was a sign above the door of the carpenter's shop in Nazareth which read, 'My yokes fit well.'

Conclusion

In summary, Jesus speaks of childlike trust in a special revelation, meditates on the content of the revelation in the relationship between Father and Son, and issues an invitation to weary and burdened people and promises rest for their souls.

John the Evangelist

Ketchikan Alaska

3 The Testament of Jesus

John 17 is like a last will and testament of Jesus for his ancient and modern followers. We learn of the glory of God the Father, the grace of Jesus the Son, and the purpose of God in the life of believers.

Introduction

The prayer of John 17 comes after Jesus has taught the disciples by deed (setting an example by washing the disciples' feet) and word (teaching the disciples about the Holy Spirit) in John 13 to 16. It also comes before Jesus dies for his disciples in John 18 to 19 and lives for his disciples in John 20 to 21.

In John 17 Jesus reveals the heights of God's provision for himself as God's Son, for his disciples as followers of Jesus, and for their successors as friends of Jesus in a hostile environment. Jesus not only explains his crisis, he also prays for his followers in their crises.

Jesus prays for himself

Father, the hour has come; glorify your Son so that the Son may glorify you, since you have given him authority over all people, to give eternal life to all whom you have given him.
 And this is eternal life, that they may know you, the
 only true God, and Jesus Christ whom you have sent.
I glorified you on earth by finishing the work that you gave me to do. So now, Father, glorify me in your own presence

29

with the glory that I had in your presence before the world existed.
(John 17: 1b-5)

Jesus addresses God as Father and speaks of glory, glory of Son and Father. Jesus has been talking with his friends about the Father in John 14 to 16, but now he talks with the Father about his friends in John 17.

The hour has come for the Son to finish the work he has been given to do. He has been doing his Father's work in the signs which are recorded in the Fourth Gospel: turning water into wine, healing a child, curing a lame man, feeding the hungry, crossing the sea, giving sight to a beggar, and raising a dead man. And now he is going to death on a cross. *Having loved his own who were in the world, he loved them to the end.(John 13:1b)*

The whole life of Jesus the Son reveals the glory of God the Father. Glory is something to be seen in Jesus. He reveals the splendour of God. Glory is to be seen in works of divine power performed by Jesus. His signs reveal the power of God. Glory will even be seen in the death of Jesus on a Roman cross outside a city wall. *For God so loved the world that he gave his only Son.(John 3:16a)*

It is no wonder that eternal life is defined in the Testament of Jesus as knowing the only true God and Jesus Christ the one sent by the Father. The sending forth of Jesus by God is a theme throughout the Gospels and the book of Acts. In John it is said over and over again: compare 3:17, 34; 5:36, 38; 6:29, 57; 7:29; 8:42; 11:42; 17:3, 8, 21, 23, 25; 20:21. The last reference links the sending of Jesus by God to the sending of the disciples by Jesus: *As the Father has sent me, so I send you. (John 20:21)*

Jesus speaks in terms of his earthly life and by prayer looks ahead to the heavenly realm which awaits beyond his arrest, the trials, his condemnation, and the crucifixion. Therefore, we see that Jesus' sense of identity and purpose has important implications for his present disciples and for future believers in him.

In praying for himself, Jesus lays the foundation for his followers to know the glory of God in their own lives: *we have seen his glory, the glory as of the Father's only Son, full of grace and truth.(John 1:14b)* In praying for himself, Jesus also gives them the possibility to share the experience of God's kind of life: *you may come to believe that Jesus is the Messiah, the Son of God, and ... through believing you may have life in his name.(John 20:31)*

Jesus prays for his disciples

I have made your name known to those whom you gave me from the world ...
the words that you gave to me I have given to them, and they have received them and know in truth that I came from you ...
I am not asking on behalf of the world, but on behalf of those whom you gave me ...
And now I am no longer in the world, but they are in the world, and I am coming to you. Holy Father, protect them in your name that you have given me, so that they may be one,

as we are one. While I was with them, I protected them in your name that you have given me ...
I speak these things in the world so that they may have my joy made complete in themselves. I have given them your word ...
I ask you to protect them from the evil one ...
Sanctify them in the truth; your word is truth ...
And for their sakes I sanctify myself, so that they also may be sanctified in truth.
(John 17: 6a, 8a, 9b, 11, 12a, 13b, 14a, 15b, 17, 19)

Yet again Jesus addresses God as Father and prays for his present disciples. Jesus has made known to them the name of God, the Holy Father. In other words, he has revealed who God truly is and what God actually does. Jesus is the self revelation of God. His disciples have received God's message in Jesus. The faith was caught by them and taught to them in the person and work of Jesus. The disciples have experienced the truth in their encounter with Jesus.

Jesus prays that the disciples may be protected from the evil one, that the joy of Jesus may be made complete in his followers, and that the disciples may be sanctified in the truth.

Although the devil is mentioned quite often in John's Gospel, this is the only place in which he is called *the evil one*. Christians need to avoid the extremes of paying too much or too little attention to the power of evil. The former can lead to a morbid fascination with the power of evil and the latter can lead to an unwillingness to acknowledge the peril of evil. The truly Christian approach is to experience the victory of Jesus over evil in his death and resurrection.

Joy is a recurring theme in John's Gospel: see 3:29; 15:11; 16:20-22, 24; 17:13. Joy is found in John the Baptist who gladly gives way to Jesus the Messiah. Joy is the gift of Jesus in the life of the believer. The joy of resurrection follows the sorrow of crucifixion. Joy is the gift of God expected in the future coming of Jesus yet experienced in the present life of faith. Christians are meant to be joyful people. A joyless Christian is a contradiction in terms.

Finally, Jesus prays that his followers may be made holy, that is, consecrated, dedicated, sanctified in the truth. Christians are set aside and made suitable for the service of God in the world by and for the truth as it is in Jesus. By and for Jesus Christians are set free to serve. They are cleansed and forgiven, they belong to God and Jesus, and they join each other in the fellowship of God's people.

The influence of Jesus on his followers reminds me of the influence of my Anglican Headmaster at Brighton Grammar. One day I was asked to report to the Head's study. He had learnt that I had been studying Greek because I was interested in becoming a minister. So it was on June 10th 1958 that Canon Wilson gave me a Greek New Testament from his private library. In so doing he proved to be a true follower of Jesus in encouraging a young Baptist student to pursue his sense of call to ministry.

Jesus prays for future believers

I ask not only on behalf of these, but also on behalf of those who will believe in me through their word, that they may all be one. As you, Father, are in me and I am in you, may they

also be in us, so that the world may believe that you have sent me ...
so that the world may know that you have sent me ...
Father, I desire that those also, whom you have given me, may be with me where I am, to see my glory ...
Righteous Father, the world does not know you, but I know you; and these know that you have sent me. I made your name known to them ...
(John 17:20-21, 23b, 24a, 25, 26a)

Once more Jesus addresses God as Father and prays for future believers in him. Negatively, the world is society organised apart from God. Positively, the unity of future believers is based on the unity of the Father and the Son. As a result, the world is to come to *believe* that God did send Jesus and to *know* that God did send Jesus, and the believers are to *see* the glory of God in Jesus. The assumption is that Jesus has made known to the believers the name of God, the Righteous Father.

Jesus looks beyond his immediate followers to those who will believe in him through their spoken and written testimony. The world will still be opposed to Jesus and his message ... but it will still be loved by God! The mutual love of Father and Son will be as strong as ever. It could be said that they are the ultimate admiration society!

In retrospect we can enlarge our understanding of such love, desire, and purpose to include all three members of the Triune Godhead. The implicit teaching of the New Testament became the explicit teaching of the Christian Church. God is rightly understood as Father (God for us and everywhere), Son (God with us and there), Spirit (God in us and here).

Conclusion

On the one hand, we see the influence of Jesus in his followers. As pastor of the local church I supported the presenters in the Christian Option Programme at a primary school at Christmas and Easter. One day I turned up and introduced myself by name to the volunteers. One of them stopped me afterwards and asked if I was related to Sue Rowston. I said that she was my first wife who had died of cancer. The volunteer then proceeded to thank me for the contribution Sue had made in the Lifeline Training Course about 25 years previously. The volunteer had been wanting to say this for a long time.

On the other hand, we note the similarities of the Testament of Jesus with the Model Prayer:
Both ask for the revelation of God's glory.
Father, glorify us in your own presence with the glory that Jesus had in your presence before the world existed.
Our Father in heaven, hallowed be your name, your kingdom come, your will be done.
Both pray for the gift of the grace of Jesus.
Holy Father, protect us in your name that you have given Jesus, so that we may be one, as God and Jesus are one.
Give us this day our daily bread, and forgive us our sins, and rescue us from the evil one.
Both look to God for achieving unity of purpose.
As you, Father, are in Jesus and Jesus is in you, may we also be in you, so that the world may believe that you have sent Jesus.
Hallowed be your name, your kingdom come, your will be done, on earth as it is in heaven.

St Paul's Outside the Walls Rome

4 The Theology of Prayer

God is like a chess grandmaster who takes into account our good and bad choices in life and fits them together so that they make a meaningful pattern. In everything the Spirit of God co-operates for good with those who love God so that his purpose is fulfilled in his people being made in the likeness of Christ.

Introduction

Paul writes his greatest letter to followers of Jesus in Rome, some of whom he knows elsewhere but many of whom he does not know. Paul shares his version of the good news about Christ, who is God's saving power and God's way of righting wrong.

In Romans 8 Paul speaks of Christian life as God's saving power at work through the Spirit of Christ. There is no condemnation for believers who experience the Spirit's law, mind set, indwelling, enlivening, leading, witness, first fruits, and intercession.

The Spirit within is our helper

Likewise the Spirit helps us in our weakness; for we do not know how to pray as we ought, but that very Spirit intercedes with sighs too deep for words. And God, who searches the heart, knows what is the mind of the Spirit, because the Spirit intercedes for the saints according to the will of God. (Romans 8:26-27)

Here is Paul's theology of prayer in the midst of life. When we pray we are not alone. Prayer is the Spirit of God at work in us and life is the Spirit of God at work with us.

Mother Teresa of Calcutta was once asked, 'When you pray, what do you say to God?' She replied, 'I say nothing. I just listen.' Then she was asked, 'What does God say to you?' She answered, 'God says nothing. He just listens ... And if you don't understand that, I can't explain it to you.' Perhaps the explanation is *sighs too deep for words*. We do not know what to pray for, what the will of God necessarily is. We can be lost for words, we can be stuck with wordless groans. Yet in and through *sighs too deep for words* the Spirit comes to the aid of our weakness. When we don't know how to pray in the face of human sickness, natural disaster, or evil activity, the Spirit of Christ pleads for us in and through *sighs too deep for words*.

We can be ignorant, short sighted, narrow minded. The Spirit of Christ is knowledgeable, long sighted, and merciful. He pleads for us according to God's wishes and desires. Yes, the Spirit within is our helper.

God above is our assurance

We know that God makes all things work together for good for those who love God, who are called according to his purpose. For those whom he foreknew he also predestined to be conformed to the image of his Son, in order that he might be the firstborn within a large family. And those whom he predestined he also called; and those whom he called he also justified; and those whom he justified he also glorified. (Romans 8:28-30)

There are three ways of interpreting Romans 8:28a.
First, if we follow the traditional reading in the NRSV, 'all things' is the subject of the verb. *We know that all things work together for good for those who love God.*
Second, if we follow the marginal reading in the NRSV, 'God' is the subject and 'all things' is the object of the clause. *We know that God makes all things work together for good for those who love God.*
Third, if we follow the translation in the Revised English Bible, 'he' is the subject and refers back to the Spirit in the previous verse. *In everything, as we know, he co-operates for good with those who love God.*

The reasoning behind accepting the second or third interpretation of Romans 8:28a is as follows. Things do not work themselves out but, left alone, they go wrong. Rather, if we love God and are receptive to his will, God and/or the Spirit of Christ, works with us in bringing about good. The good things are described in what follows, *to be conformed to the image of his Son*, being made in the likeness of Christ.

We do not give thanks **for** all things but **in** all things. As Paul said elsewhere, *Pray without ceasing, give thanks in all circumstances; for this is the will of God in Christ Jesus for you.(1 Thessalonians 5:17-18)* We do not give thanks for human sickness, natural disaster, or evil activity. However, we may give thanks in all things for God's gifts which create and sustain, restore and renew.

Paul assures us about the outworking of God's purpose. God *foreknew, predestined, called, justified,* and *glorified.* These terms are shaped by the personal revelation of God in Christ.

God is recreating humanity in the image of his Son. God knows the goal to which he is bringing his creation. God has a plan for the fullness of time, to gather up all things in Christ (Ephesians 1:10).

In the story of creation, *God created humankind in his image, in the image of God he created them; male and female he created them.(Genesis 1:27)* The creation is paralleled by the new creation in the New Testament. *It is the God who said, "Let light shine out of darkness," who has shone in our hearts to give the light of the knowledge of the glory of God in the face of Jesus Christ.(2 Corinthians 4:6)* In Jesus, God above is our assurance.

Conclusion

Some years ago a grieving widower was preparing the evening meal for his two young children. He stood at the kitchen bench and was listening to the radio when he heard the words of a song sung by Art Garfunkel: *Bright eyes burning like fire, Bright eyes how can you close and fail? How can the light that burned so brightly suddenly burn so pale? Bright eyes.*

In and through *sighs too deep for words* the Spirit came to the aid of his weakness. As his eyes filled with tears he felt the everlasting arms of God lifting him up to complete the menial tasks which confronted him in the care of his children.

In life and death Jesus sensed his Father at work in all that he encountered. We too can be truly Christlike when we learn to face the good and bad and to experience the Spirit of Christ co-operating for good in all things.

5 The Prayer of the Trinity

The grace of our Lord Jesus Christ,
in which the love of God is exercised,
and the communion of the Spirit disclosed and imparted,
be with you all.
Karl Barth's translation of 2 Corinthians 13:13

Introduction

A popular psychologist on television often asks his troubled guests, 'How's it working for you?' He challenges them to think of better ways of coping with life. The same challenge confronts us too as we face expected or unexpected upturns or downturns physically, or emotionally, or intellectually, or financially, or spiritually.

Paul could have given an interesting response to such an enquiry in 2 Corinthians 10-13. His readers were facing a negative future threatened by false preachers. Paul himself was facing a range of issues including *weaknesses, insults, hardships, persecutions, and calamities.(2 Corinthians 12:10)*

Yet Paul's prayer for his readers and himself is positive:

The grace of the Lord Jesus Christ,
the love of God,
and the communion of the Holy Spirit be with all of you.
(2 Corinthians 13:13)

A technicality in the original Greek
Option 1 Three subjective genitives - *grace, love, communion* come from God.
Option 2 Two subjective genitives - *grace* & *love* come from Jesus and God - and one objective genitive - *communion* is in the Spirit.

The grace of the Lord Jesus Christ

Paul's prays for the action and gift of Christ to be extended towards his readers. Paul had been a persecutor of Christians before he became a Christian. When he was converted he sensed God's free unmerited favour in Christ and said, *By the grace of God I am what I am, and his grace toward me has not been in vain.(1 Corinthians 15:10)* God showed Paul his kindness in Christ and set Paul free from his sinful pride as a self righteous persecutor.

Elie Wiesel is a Jewish survivor of the Nazi holocaust. In his book *Night*, the Hungarian Jew tells his story. As a child Elie Wiesel experienced the horrors of Nazi concentration camps. On one occasion Hitler's special police hanged two Jewish men and a young boy in front of the whole camp. The men died quickly, but the death throes of the youth lasted for half an hour. 'For God's sake, where is God?' someone asked behind Elie. He heard a voice answer: 'Where is he? This is where - hanging here on the gallows . . .' To a Christian, Wiesel's story recalls the grace of the crucified Jesus.

The love of God

Paul also prays for the love of God to be known by his readers. Later, in his letter to Rome Paul says two important things. The **revelation** of God's love is through the historical event of the death of Jesus: *God proves his love for us in that while we still were sinners Christ died for us.(Romans 5:8)* The **application** of God's love is by the Spirit of Jesus: *God's love has been poured into our hearts through the Holy Spirit that has been given to us.(Romans 5:5)*

The story is told of a young minister who became concerned about an older married couple. The wife was the most active and generous person in his church. The husband never came to church, he did nothing for it, he gave nothing to it. As time went by, he said to himself, 'I have got to do something about this man.' He made an appointment and met the businessman at his office. The older man sat behind his desk and listened as the young minister spoke falteringly about the Christian faith. When he finished, there was silence. So the young man started again. After the second time, the older man just sat there. Then the young minister tried a third time. When he finished, he wished that he had never come. But the businessman wrote a note on a pad and passed it to him. It read: 'I am so moved that I cannot speak.' It was the first time that an adult had spoken frankly to him about faith in Christ. That businessman became a Christian and joined his wife in experiencing the love of God as a member of the body of Christ. We are reminded of 'the Gospel in miniature': *God so loved the world that he gave his only Son, so that everyone who believes in him may not perish but may have eternal life.(John 3:16)*

The communion of the Holy Spirit

Finally, Paul prays for the communion created by the Spirit among his readers, or for the participation of the readers in the Spirit. In an earlier letter to the Corinthians Paul had spoken of the fellowship that comes from the Spirit or the sharing that goes to the Spirit: *In the one Spirit we were all baptized into one body ... and we were all made to drink of one Spirit ... Now you are the body of Christ and individually members of it.(1 Corinthians 12:13, 27)* If we belong to God in Christ by the Spirit, then we belong to God's people. This is something that nobody can deny.

Rita Snowden tells how she visited a small town near the white cliffs of Dover. She was having afternoon tea in a cafe when she became aware of a beautiful scent filling the atmosphere. She asked the waiter about the source of the wondrous scent and was told that it came from people passing by. They worked in a perfume factory down the road and were walking home. When the workers left the factory they carried with them the fragrance which had permeated their workday clothes. The moral was clear. Christians should allow themselves in Sunday worship to be permeated with the sweetness of God's presence. Then as they go about their weekday activities the fragrance of the Lord goes with them and all the people they meet become aware of God's fragrance.

Conclusion
Paul's benediction is about trinitarian values and is in line with the order of Christian experience. It begins with the *grace* of Christ. Through Christ's grace Christians learn of the Father's *love* and experience the Spirit's *communion*.

6 The Testament of Paul

Whether we go forward or backward, up to the heights or down to the depths, nothing will be able to separate us from the love of God in Christ Jesus our Lord.

Introduction

In Ephesians chapters 1 to 3, at the end of his explanation of what God has done for his people in Christ, Paul writes his last will and testament for his readers. It comes in the form of a prayer. The prayer answers three questions.

To whom do we pray?

For this reason I bow my knees before the Father, from whom every family in heaven and on earth takes its name. (Ephesians 3:14-15)

There is a play on words in the Greek: *Father ... family*. The divine fatherhood is the origin of each and every family. All families are united under the Father of Jesus Christ. We are praying to the God who unites us.

Previously Paul had written about Jesus who is our peace and how he has broken down the dividing wall, that is, the hostility between us. Paul had noted the purpose of God through Christ to create one new humanity and to reconcile different groups to God in one body through the cross (Ephesians 2:14-16). We pray to the God who unites us.

What do we pray?

I pray that, according to the riches of his glory, he may grant that you may be strengthened in your inner being with power through his Spirit, and that Christ may dwell in your hearts through faith, as you are being rooted and grounded in love.
I pray that you may have the power to comprehend, with all the saints, what is the breadth and length and height and depth, and to know the love of Christ that surpasses knowledge, so that you may be filled with all the fullness of God.(Ephesians 3:16-19)

God's saving power is not an abstraction but it comes as Christ becomes a transforming presence within the inner self. We are praying that we shall be changed daily by Christ within us. In another letter Paul went so far as to say that the secret of the followers of Jesus was to have Christ in us. 'And the secret is simply this: Christ *in you*! Yes, Christ *in you* bringing with him the hope of all the glorious things to come.' (Colossians 1:27 Phillips) We pray that we shall be changed daily by Christ within us. This is not an understanding for a solitary person but is the experience of those who learn *with all the saints*. The motto, 'United we stand, divided we fall,' rings true.

There is a contrast between the followers of Jesus as they should be and the world outside Christ as it is. If Christians tolerate the same divisions of class or race or colour or creed as non Christians, their witness is compromised and amounts to nothing. There is also a challenge to all the followers of Jesus. Christians should not cut themselves off from the illumination which comes from other Christians with different backgrounds or nationalities or cultures.

The motivation, of course, is *the love of Christ*, possibly meaning love for Christ (objective genitive), but more likely meaning Christ's love for us (subjective genitive). Christ's love comes in four dimensions.

The love Christ has for us is **so broad** that it encompasses the whole world. When Karl Barth, the greatest Christian thinker of the twentieth century, was preaching his last sermons, it was in a Swiss prison. He told the inmates that the four words 'My grace is enough' in 2 Corinthians 12:9 'say much more and say it better than the whole pile of paper with which I have surrounded myself. They are enough - something that I am very far from being able to say about my books.'

The love Christ has for us is **so long** that it goes to the very end. A woman went Christmas shopping with her two children. After going to and fro in a large department store, she was exhausted. She dragged herself and the two children with all the bags of shopping into a lift. When the lift doors closed she couldn't stand it anymore and she said out loud, 'Whoever started this whole Christmas thing should be found, strung up, and executed!' From the back of the lift a voice calmly responded, 'Don't worry, we have already crucified him.' The rest of the trip to the ground floor was so quiet that you could hear a pin drop.

The love Christ has for us is **so high** that it reaches the very best. A former editor of *The Southern Cross* recalls working with Sister Angela, an Irish Dominican nun, who had been a secondary teacher before she served as a librarian and an archivist between the ages of 61 and 89. 'It was an unexpected blessing,' writes Matthew Abraham. 'When friends in the secular media would ask me what life was like working for the church, I could honestly tell them that my office came complete with its very own angel ... She was devout, intelligent and always great fun.'

The love Christ has for us is **so deep** that it seeks the very worst. Edward VIII has been described by Alistair Cooke as "a charming, spoiled, woefully ill-educated man, painfully simple-minded and ferociously acquisitive. He is more to be pitied than abused in that the worlds of art, literature, music, politics, science, religion, philosophy . . . were closed to him. At the end . . . 'he had three interests - golf, gardening, and money . . . and the greatest of these was money.' "

Christ's love also brings an **overwhelming** experience. It is a matter of experiencing it more than thinking about it. Ron Difrancesco was at his desk on the 84th floor of the south tower of the World Trade Centre in New York City when the hijacked plane struck the north tower on September 11 2001 at 8 46 am. He stayed at his desk until he was persuaded to leave by a friend who rang him from Toronto.

As he walked towards the lifts, the second hijacked plane hit the south tower at 9 03 am. The trading floor he had just left no longer existed. Ron made his way to one of three emergency stairwells, the only one that offered hope of escape for people above the point of impact. He proceeded down until he was told to go back up due to smoke and fire. He went a little way up and then turned around and started to go down again. At one point he stopped and lay down with others who were overcome by the smoke. He saw people crying, people panicking, people unconscious.

Then he heard a voice saying, 'Get up, Ron! Hey! You can do this.' Ron sensed being lifted up, guided, and led. He saw and followed a ray of light. He encountered flames but someone helped him through. Finally, he reached a clear stairwell below the fire on the 76th floor. Only then did the sense of the helper who had been with him for five minutes end. Ron Difrancisco was the last person out of the south tower before it collapsed at 9 59 am. He was one of only four people to escape from above the 81st floor of the south tower. He can't understand why he survived when many others perished but he attributes his escape to divine intervention. We may not know the love of Christ so dramatically but we can know the love Christ has for us day by day.

What are the outcomes of our prayer?

Now to him who by the power at work within us is able to accomplish abundantly far more than all we can ask or imagine, to him be glory in the church and in Christ Jesus to all generations, for ever and ever. Amen.(Ephesians 3:20-21)

Paul presents a majestic vision of God as Father of the family members who follow Jesus. Paul makes huge requests to God that we shall be transformed and united and motivated. Paul does so because God's powerful activity is not limited by our impoverished imagination or by our petty prayers. We can be links in the chain of God's great work in the church and in Christ Jesus!

Conclusion

We pray to the God who unites us. We pray that we shall be changed daily by Christ within us, united as followers of Jesus, and motivated by the love of Christ for us. We pray to the God and Father of our Lord Jesus Christ who can do more than we ask or imagine.

Paul the Apostle Rome

7 The God of Peace

In the mind of the author of Hebrews preaching and teaching the Christian faith is the endeavour to help needy people by telling them what the Old Testament says about their high priest and shepherd, Jesus Christ.

Introduction

At the end of the Letter to the Hebrews is a truly great prayer. The Letter may well be a collection of sermons. It would be most appropriate for the unknown preacher to conclude with a blessing upon his original listeners and his subsequent readers.

Now may the God of peace, who brought back from the dead our Lord Jesus, the great shepherd of the sheep, by the blood of the eternal covenant, make you complete in everything good so that you may do his will, working among us that which is pleasing in his sight, through Jesus Christ, to whom be the glory for ever and ever. Amen.(Hebrews 13:20-21)

Climax of the Covenant

Jesus is seen as the fulfilment of the promises of God and so Hebrews includes teaching about Jesus in the light of the Old Testament:
Jesus, God's final revelation, is better than the angels;
Jesus, pioneer of salvation, is better than Moses;
Jesus, great high priest, is better than the earthly high priest;
Jesus, priestly king of a new order, mediates a better covenant;

Jesus, pioneer and perfecter of faith, embodies something better.

The link between Christian teaching and Christian living is Jesus and so Hebrews gives a series of warnings about continuing as faithful believers:
Beware of drifting away, of drifting from your course.
Beware of hardening your hearts, of growing stubborn.
Beware of becoming sluggish, being lax, or becoming lazy.
Beware of shrinking back and being lost.
Beware of refusing to hear the message of God.

After Hebrews has alternated between teachings about Jesus Christ and challenges about Christian living, the book's argument comes to a fitting climax in its beautiful benediction.

The anonymous author prays to *the God of peace* whose power is evident in the resurrection of Jesus. Jesus himself is *the great shepherd* and has inaugurated by his death *the eternal covenant*. The preacher prays for the completing of *everything good*, with a view to the doing of God's *will*, by means of the working of what is *pleasing* to God. This is all *through Jesus Christ*. He is the one to whom *the glory* belongs, the one in whom God's covenant with humanity comes to its climax.

Peace and Power

The God of peace is the God of power in Old and New Testaments. Peace is the well-being and salvation of human beings body and soul. Well-being and wholeness is the work of God. It is known through the exodus under the leadership of Moses, *the one who brought them up out of the sea with the shepherds of his flock.(Isaiah 63:11)* It is also known through the resurrection of Jesus. *The God of peace ... brought back from the dead our Lord Jesus.*

Jesus is called *a great high priest* in Hebrews 4 and *the great shepherd of the sheep* in Hebrews 13. In both cases it is because of *the blood of the eternal covenant.* The high priest presents the perfect sacrifice and the shepherd is willing to lay down his life for his flock. The Old Testament gives God's promise: *I will make with you an everlasting covenant.(Isaiah 55:3)* The New Testament tells us that God keeps his promise: *This cup is the new covenant in my blood.(1 Corinthians 11:25)*

The God of peace is the God of power through Christ in the lives of Christians. The preacher prays that God may *make you complete in everything good.* The verb *make complete* can be translated *make perfect.* The verb is used of fishermen *mending* their nets in Mark 1:19. Being made complete or perfect can include being mended by God.

The prayer for completion or perfection has a purpose: *so that you may do his* (God's) *will.* The prayer also has a means of completing or perfecting: (God is) *working among us that which is pleasing in his sight.* We are unable to be made complete or perfect in our own strength. Donald Coggan has written, 'We set the sail of our will; He fills it with the wind of His Spirit.'

The preacher concludes the prayer by noting that *the glory* is given to *the God of peace* through *our Lord Jesus.* Indeed, the benediction ends with *the glory for ever and ever* where the writer began his Letter, with Jesus the Son of God sitting *at the right hand of the Majesty on high.(Hebrews 1:3)*

Conclusion

Steve Chalke once had a speaking engagement in a 900 year old heritage listed church building. The stone building was cool during summer but freezing during winter. The congregation decided to install a specially designed set of radiators at a huge cost in terms of their budget. Steve heard about the radiators as he waited to speak. It was cold and he tentatively asked if the radiators could be turned on. The vicar took Steve through the vast building and traced the pipe that connected the radiators together.

In a small back room he saw the end of the pipe. It just stopped. The people had been so taken by the beautiful design of the heating system and the hope of being warm during winter that no one bothered to think about whether they were connected to the gas main or not. The heating system looked state of the art, but actually it was useless. It wasn't connected to anything at all. God in Christ is the provider of saving power and the enabler of Christian living. True believers need to be connected to God by faith and obedience.

8 The God of Grace and Glory

The First Letter of Peter balances the indicative of the Good News with the imperative of the Good News. It teaches readers about the living hope, God's own people, and Christian suffering. It also encourages readers to be holy, to submit to legitimate authority, and to exercise pastoral care.

Introduction

At the end of a letter which acknowledges the calling of Christians to be true to their Lord in the face of possible or actual opposition, there is a fine prayer for us to make our own.

And after you have suffered for a little while, the God of all grace, who has called you to his eternal glory in Christ, will himself restore, support, strengthen, and establish you. To him be the power for ever and ever. Amen. (1 Peter 5:10-11)

In a Time of Suffering

The First Letter of Peter is directed towards believers in the northern area of Asia Minor. It is likely that the letter is written by Peter with the secretarial support of Silvanus before the Great Fire of Rome in AD 64. After the fire Nero shifted the blame for it from himself to the Christians and had many of them executed, including Paul by beheading and Peter by crucifixion. One part of the letter (1 Peter 1:3 to 4:11) seems to consider persecution to be only a possibility for some readers, whereas another part of the letter (1 Peter 4:12 to 5:11) appears to admit persecution to be an actuality for other readers.

Prayer of Praise

The short prayer at the end of 1 Peter takes the experience of suffering seriously. In the long term suffering is seen to be *for a little while (1 Peter 1:6; 5:10)* and is endured because *Christ suffered (1 Peter 2:21; 3:18)*. Indeed, Peter speaks of *sharing Christ's sufferings* with rejoicing and of suffering *as a Christian* to *glorify God (1 Peter 4:13, 16)*. Peter himself is *a witness of the sufferings of Christ* and *one who shares in the glory to be revealed(1 Peter 5:1)*.

Three attributes of God are the basis of the prayer:
Grace is the free unmerited favour of God revealed in Jesus Christ by whom God sets us free from sin and puts us into right relationship with himself. Peter prays to *the God of all grace*.

Glory is the radiant splendour of God's active presence revealed in the person and work of Jesus Christ. Accordingly, Peter speaks of God's **eternal** *glory in Christ.*

Power is the mighty strength, the ruling might, the lasting sovereignty of the creating and redeeming God revealed in Jesus Christ.

The words of Harry Emerson Fosdick's hymn are most apt:
'God of grace and God of glory, on your people pour your power.'

At first the prayer looked backward: God *has called you*. Then it looks forward: God *will ... restore, support, strengthen, and establish you*.

Four strong verbs of promise would have encouraged the first readers or listeners. They certainly provide readers in modern times with true encouragement.

Restore means 'cause to be in a condition to function well, prepare for a purpose'. As we noted previously, in Hebrews 13:21 it is translated *make complete* and it is used of fishermen *mending* their nets in Mark 1:19.

Support means literally 'fix firmly in place' and metaphorically 'cause to be inwardly firm or committed'.

Strengthen means 'make strong' and it appears only here in the New Testament.

Establish means literally 'provide a base for some material object or structure' and metaphorically 'provide a secure basis for the inner life and its resources' . It is used of the believers whom God establishes. Elsewhere, believers are said to be established in *love* (Ephesians 3:17) and in *the faith* (Colossians 1:23).

Conclusion

It seems likely when Peter's little prayer was read aloud in the early churches that the listeners would join in saying 'Amen', meaning 'Let it be' at the end. So may we.

A Benediction

*Christ go before you,
to prepare a way of service;
Christ go behind you,
to gather up your efforts for his glory;
Christ go beside you,
as leader and guide;
Christ go within you,
as comfort and stay;
Christ go beneath you,
to uphold with everlasting arms;
Christ go above you,
to reign as Lord supreme.*

William E. Hull

9 The Presence of God

And now unto him who is able to keep us from falling and lift us from the dark valley of despair to the bright mountain of hope, from the midnight of desperation to the daybreak of joy; to him be power and authority, for ever and ever. Amen.
Martin Luther King's paraphrase of Jude 24-25

Introduction

Some years ago I called the Letter of Jude 'The Most Neglected Book in the New Testament'. Although the academic world has started to remedy this situation with learned articles and detailed commentaries, it is probably still true that the average churchgoer or Bible reader is only acquainted with two things in the book.

First, Jude makes **a plea** *to contend for the faith that was once for all entrusted to the saints.(Jude 3)* It is worth considering Jude's predicament. Second, Jude says **a prayer** *to him who is able to keep you from falling ... (Jude 24-25)* It is also worth analysing Jude's prayer of praise:
   Now to him who is able to keep you from falling,
   and to make you stand without blemish
   in the presence of his glory with rejoicing,
   to the only God our Saviour,
   through Jesus Christ our Lord,
   be glory, majesty, power, and authority,
   before all time and now and for ever. Amen.
   (Jude 24-25)

Jude's Predicament

Before the end of the first century, Jude criticised opponents who were morally lax and somewhat rationalistic. Jude's opponents divorced their beliefs from their morals just as gnostics would do in the second century.

Jude warns Christians confronting moral laxity in the activity of *ungodly* people *who pervert the grace of our God into licentiousness and deny our only Master and Lord, Jesus Christ.(Jude 4)*

Jude gives strong words to believers who were facing rationalistic thinking. He reminds his readers of coming judgement in a quotation from a noncanonical Jewish source: *See, the Lord is coming ... to execute judgement on all, and to convict everyone of all the deeds of ungodliness ... (Jude 14-15)* Jude also quotes a prediction which is attributed to the apostles of the Lord: *In the last time there will be scoffers, indulging their own ungodly lusts.(Jude 18)*

Jude seeks to provide remedies for false beliefs and unhelpful practices by mentioning positive Christian elements:
*Build yourselves up on your most holy faith;
pray in the Holy Spirit;
keep yourselves in the love of God;
look forward to the mercy of our Lord Jesus Christ
that leads to eternal life.
(Jude 20-21)*

Jude also stresses divine help in his closing prayer of praise.

Jude's Prayer

Jude's magnificent prayer of praise is in four parts.

The person to be praised

The only God our Saviour is praised because he is able to guard and keep believers from stumbling or falling and because he is able to present and make believers stand unblemished or without reproach. God does this both here and hereafter. Believers anticipate by faith the joyfulness and celebration of the glorious presence of God.

The words by which praise is spoken

Glory or divine radiance, majesty or divine transcendence, power or divine creativity, and authority or victorious freedom - these attributes are ascribed to the only God our Saviour through Jesus the Christ our Lord. When the first century believers ascribed glory to God, they did so through Jesus, the human face of God.

The times in which praise is due

Glory, majesty, power, and authority belong to God before all time, now, and for ever. A generation before Jude's Letter a similar understanding was expressed in Paul's greatest letter. *For from him and through him and to him are all things. To him be the glory for ever. Amen.(Romans 11:36)* God's greatness is acknowledged from the beginning to end of history.

The response of people who hear the praise

It seems likely when Jude's Letter was read aloud in the early churches the listeners would join in saying 'Amen' at the end of the prayer of praise. 'Amen' is a Greek word from Hebrew and means 'So be it' or 'Let it be'.

Jude's prayer of praise provides believers with an antidote to misunderstandings of religious beliefs and practices.

The one and only God is recognised as the one who is able to keep us from falling out of grace into disgrace and to present us unblemished as living sacrifices in this world and the next.

Jesus is acknowledged as **the one and only mediator** who brings our prayerful praises to God. The attributes of glory, majesty, power, and authority belong to the Lord of history before time began, in the present age, and to all eternity.

The ancient world had its fair share of religious options. For example, in the second century there were full blown systems of Gnosticism. They valued *gnosis*, special knowledge, by which access was gained to the saving power of the superior god beyond the material world which had been created by an inferior god.

If Jude's opponents had gnostic leanings, the emphases of the closing prayer of praise would counteract such false religiosity.

The modern world also has its fair share of understandings of God which vary from the Pantheism of Hinduism, the Cosmic Order of Buddhism, the Monotheism of Judaism, the Trinitarian Theism of Christianity, the Sovereignty of Islam, to the Non-existent God of Atheism.

Jude's prayer certainly leads us in the direction of the One God, the One Mediator, and the Creator and the Redeemer for time and eternity.

Conclusion

The present experience that God provides believers is to be strengthened by the one who is able to keep them from falling.

The ultimate hope that God provides believers is to stand rejoicing without sin and without fear in his presence.

The God who provides this sort of present and future is the one to whom belong power and authority before all time and now and for ever.

Mother and Child
Hagia Sophia Istanbul

10 The Saviour

Mary's song about the Saviour is traditionally called the *Magnificat*. *Magnificare* meaning 'to think much of' was the Latin infinitive of the Greek verb translated *magnifies* in the song.

Introduction

The first two chapters of Luke's Gospel are like a modern musical. Whenever something important comes to pass somebody bursts into song. We shall look at three of these songs.

Elizabeth, the expectant mother of John the Baptist, has just praised Mary, the soon to be mother of her Lord and Messiah, in Luke 1:42-45. Mary then praises God her Saviour because *he has looked with favour on the lowliness of his servant.* She sounds like Hannah, the mother of the prophet Samuel, in 1 Samuel 2:1-10.

Mary's Individual Thanksgiving

My soul magnifies the Lord,
and my spirit rejoices in God my Saviour,
for he has looked with favour on the lowliness of his servant.
Surely, from now on all generations will call me blessed;
for the Mighty One has done great things for me,
and holy is his name. (Luke 1:46-49)

Hannah's song had begun joyfully: *My heart exults in the Lord; my strength is exalted in my God ... because I rejoice in your salvation.(1 Samuel 2:1 Greek)*

Mary's song also begins with her personal experience of joy. She *magnifies* or extols *the Lord*. She *rejoices* or begins to exult *in God* whom she calls *my Saviour.* In the Greek version of the Old Testament *Saviour* is used 35 times of God and only 5 times of a human being.

For example, the Psalmist had chanted, *They (the righteous) will receive blessing from the Lord, and mercy from God their Saviour.(Psalm 24:5 Greek)* Isaiah of Babylon had also said, *Behold, my God is my Saviour; I will trust in him, and not be afraid, for the Lord is my glory and my praise, and has become my salvation.(Isaiah 12:2 Greek)*

Mary then gives the grounds for praising God as she specifies herself as the object of divine grace. God has regarded or *looked with favour on the lowliness* or humble state *of his servant* or female slave. For, behold, *from now on all generations will call me blessed.* It is said of God in Old Testament times: *God ... has done for you these great and awesome things that your own eyes have seen.(Deuteronomy 10:21)* Likewise, Mary's song says: *the Mighty One has done great things for me.*

Mary's General Thanksgiving

His mercy is for those who fear him
from generation to generation.
He has shown strength with his arm;

he has scattered the proud in the thoughts of their hearts.
He has brought down the powerful from their thrones,
and lifted up the lowly;
he has filled the hungry with good things,
and sent the rich away empty.
He has helped his servant Israel,
in remembrance of his mercy,
according to the promise he made to our ancestors,
to Abraham and to his descendants forever.(Luke 1:50-55)

Mary's thoughts move from God's might to God's *mercy* or gracious faithfulness. *His mercy is for those who fear him from generation to generation.* The word translated *mercy* is the word used in the Greek Old Testament to translate the Hebrew word for *steadfast love.* The God of Israel is the God of Jesus: *a God merciful and gracious, slow to anger, and abounding in steadfast love and faithfulness, keeping steadfast love for the thousandth generation.(Exodus 34: 6-7a)*

Hannah's song had included references to the sovereignty of God: *The Lord makes poor and makes rich; he brings low, and lifts up. He lifts up the poor from the earth; he lifts the needy from the ash heap, to make them sit with the princes of the people and inherit a throne of glory.(1 Samuel 2:7-8 Greek)*

Mary's song proceeds to describe the general pattern of God's activity in a similar way. There are seven verbs in the Greek aorist tense: *He has shown ... he has scattered ... he has brought down ... (he has) lifted up ... he has filled ... (he has) sent ... away ... he has helped ...*

First, these verbs may express past events, the aorist as simple past. Second, these verbs may describe God's customary way of acting, the so called gnomic aorist. Third, these verbs may treat the future as already present, the proleptic use of the aorist. My preference is the third.

What God has begun to do in the coming of the Messiah is looked at in two ways. On the one hand, it is in tune with what God actually did in Old Testament times. On the other hand, what God actually will do in Jesus and his followers is as good as done.

Jesus brings a moral revolution. God *has shown strength with his arm; he has scattered the proud in the thoughts of their hearts.* The proud look down on other people because they don't look up to God and pride comes before a fall.

Jesus brings a social revolution. God *has brought down the powerful from their thrones, and lifted up the lowly.* The overthrow of ungodly rulers is a sign of God at work in both ancient and modern times.

Jesus brings an economic revolution. God *has filled the hungry with good things, and sent the rich away empty.* The ordinary life of human beings is meant to be brought into line with the justice of God.

Because he remembers his covenant with Abraham and his descendants, God *has helped his servant Israel.* It had been said, *Abraham shall become a great and mighty nation, and all the nations of the earth shall be blessed in him.(Genesis 18:16)* It would later be said, *Just as Abraham "believed God, and it was reckoned to him as righteousness," so, you see, those who believe are the descendants of Abraham. (Galatians 3:6-7)*

Conclusion

Mary's song is a joyful celebration of God at the coming of the Son of God and the Descendant of David. She hears, accepts, shares, and interprets the good news personally and generally. In Christian history it is a long way from the New Testament portrait of the mother of Jesus to later theological interpretations which arise out of popular devotional practices focussed on Mary.

The Council of Ephesus in 431 called her 'Mother of God'. However, it should be noted that the debate was more about Jesus' divinity than Mary's identity.

In 1854 Pope Pius IX taught the doctrine of the immaculate conception of Mary at the beginning of her life. Nearly a century later, Pope Pius XII, in 1950, taught the doctrine of the bodily assumption of Mary at the end of her life. One is hard pressed to find justification for these papal dogmas in the New Testament records.

On the other hand, in Christian hymnody it is a short way from Mary's song in Luke's Gospel to the splendid rendition of 'Tell out, my soul' by Timothy Dudley-Smith. The good bishop's version of the Magnificat is based on Luke 1:46-55 in the New English Bible. The words are sung to 'Woodlands,' the stirring tune composed by Walter Greatorex. As we sing, we tell out 'the greatness of the Lord,' 'the greatness of his name,' 'the greatness of his might,' and 'the glories of his word.' Dudley-Smith's hymn captures the spirit of Mary's song for modern believers who seek to follow Mary's example as a disciple of her son.

Luke the Evangelist Rome

11 The Prophet of The Most High

Zechariah's song about the prophet of the Most High is traditionally called the *Benedictus*. It is the past participle of the Latin verb *benedicere* meaning 'to speak well of' and is the equivalent of the Greek adjective translated *Blessed* in the song.

Introduction

In the last section of Luke 1 another important thing comes to pass - the birth and naming of John the Baptist - and another person bursts into song. The father of the Baptist, Zechariah, is released from his temporary inability to speak. He declares in an inspired song the saving will of the Most High.

A week after his birth, the boy is to be circumcised and named. Contrary to expectations, Elizabeth and Zechariah call him John, a name which is related to a Hebrew name meaning 'The Lord's gracious gift'.

Zechariah sings in praise of the God of Israel and in honour of the prophet of the Most High. His song makes allusions to the Old Testament with ideas of blessing, looking favourably, redeeming, saving, remembering, going before, forgiving, breaking upon, giving light, and guiding.

In Praise of God

Blessed be the Lord God of Israel,
for he has looked favourably on his people and redeemed them.
He has raised up a mighty saviour for us
in the house of his servant David,
as he spoke through the mouth of his holy prophets from of old,
that we would be saved from our enemies
and from the hand of all who hate us.
Thus he has shown the mercy promised to our ancestors,
and has remembered his holy covenant,
the oath that he swore to our ancestor Abraham, to grant us
that we, being rescued from the hands of our enemies,
might serve him without fear, in holiness and righteousness
before him all our days.
(Luke 1:68-75)

The form of the word *Blessed* is only used of God in the New Testament. He alone is worthy of all praise. Zechariah praises God that there have been past times of divine visitation. The Lord visited or looked in on his people (*has looked favourably on his people*); the same work of God goes on in the birth of John the predecessor of the Messiah.

The Lord is said to have *redeemed* his people. The idea goes back to the setting free of God's people at the Exodus in the time of Moses. Subsequent acts of liberation were also seen as redemption, such as the New Exodus in the return from the exile in Babylon. A further act of redemption has begun in the birth of the Baptist.

Zechariah is then depicted as knowing that Mary will give birth to *a mighty saviour*. Literally, the Greek reads 'a horn of salvation'. A horn in the Old Testament is a metaphor for strength. The picture comes from a fighting animal's erect horns and the horns on a conquering warrior's helmet. The *mighty saviour* is the descendant of King David.

In accord with the teaching of the prophets, salvation involves being rescued from hateful enemies. God has shown mercy promised to the ancestors. God has remembered the holy covenant sealed by oath with Abraham. God has given us the privilege to serve him in piety and justice our whole life long.

In Honour of the Prophet

And you, child, will be called the prophet of the Most High;
for you will go before the Lord to prepare his ways,
to give knowledge of salvation to his people
by the forgiveness of their sins.
By the tender mercy of our God,
the dawn from on high will break upon us,
to give light to those who sit in darkness
and in the shadow of death,
to guide our feet into the way of peace.
(Luke 1:76-79)

The son of Elizabeth and Zechariah is to be identified as *the prophet of the Most High*. Two infinitives describe the purpose of their son John the Baptist. He is *to prepare* a path for God's Messiah. He is *to give* an experience of God's saving power by baptizing for the remission of sins.

Zechariah praises God that there will be future times of divine visitation. The Lord *will break upon us*, that is to say, will visit or look in on us. God's work in John the Baptist will be comprehensively continued in Jesus the Messiah.

Zechariah is depicted as describing the coming Messiah as *the dawn from on high*. Literally, the Greek reads 'the rising (of the sun)' or 'the growing or shooting (of a plant)'.

The first reading of the Greek ('rising') recalls a passage about the star of Jacob in Numbers: *a star shall come out of Jacob, and a sceptre shall rise out of Israel.(Numbers 24:17)* The second reading of the Greek ('growing or shooting') recalls a passage about the shoot from David in Isaiah: *A shoot shall come out from the stump of Jesse, and a branch shall grow out of his roots.(Isaiah 11:1)* Two images which were interpreted of the Messiah are combined in Zechariah's song.

Two infinitives describe the purpose of Jesus the Messiah. He is *to give light* to people in the dark and in the face of death. He is *to guide* or direct towards the way that leads to peace.

There are parallels in the Old Testament. Isaiah of Jerusalem speaks of darkness and light: *The people who walked in darkness have seen a great light; those who lived in a land of deep darkness—on them light has shined.(Isaiah 9:2)* The Shepherd Psalm refers to the divine presence in the face of the unknown: *Even though I walk through the darkest valley, I fear no evil; for you are with me.(Psalm 23:4)* Isaiah of Jerusalem also portrays a Messiah like David: *Wonderful Counsellor, Mighty God, Everlasting Father, Prince of Peace.(Isaiah 9:6)*

Conclusion

Zechariah has sung in praise of the God of Israel and in honour of the prophet of the Most High. In the past God has dealt with Abraham and David. In the present God gives the predecessor of the Messiah. In the future God's Messiah will fulfil the hopes and dispel the fears of all who call upon the Lord.

Zechariah's song reflects on the ideas underlying the whole Bible. Tom Wright's *The Last Word* sketches **Five Acts** of the Bible's Big Story.

> **The First Act is Genesis 1 and 2.** God creates everything. God sustains everything.
> **The Second Act is Genesis 3 to 11.** The Good Story becomes Bad. People sin. God judges. Yet God rescues.
> **The Third Act begins in Genesis 12.** The Third Act goes from Father Abraham to Jesus the Messiah. God makes a promise of Something Better.
> **The Fourth Act is the Gospels.** God keeps his promise in Someone Better, Jesus the Messiah.
> **The Fifth Act is the Acts of the Apostles, the Letters, and the Revelation.** The followers of Jesus spread the story of their Saviour by their words and deeds in the power of God's Spirit. By grace through faith we live in the Fifth Act of the Bible's Story.

We participate in this Big Story as we join in Zechariah's song and express with him our thanksgiving that God has visited and redeemed his people.

Christ the King   St Augustine's   Victor Harbor

12 The Master

Simeon's song is traditionally called the *Nunc Dimittis*. *Nunc* is the Latin adverb meaning 'now'. *Dimittis* is from the Latin verb *Dimittere* meaning 'to send away, dismiss' and is the equivalent of the Greek verb translated *you are dismissing* in the song.

Master, now you are dismissing your servant in peace,
according to your word;
for my eyes have seen your salvation,
which you have prepared in the presence of all peoples,
a light for revelation to the Gentiles
and for glory to your people Israel.
(Luke 2:29-32)

Introduction
In the middle of Luke 2 an important thing comes to pass - the presentation of Jesus in the temple - and yet another person bursts into song. An old man named Simeon sees before him the fulfilment of his hopes, takes the baby Jesus in his arms, and praises God in a short but effective prayer.

Promises to Keep
According to Luke, a week after his birth, the baby is to be circumcised, named Jesus, and presented to God in the temple. The parents and the child are met by Simeon. Luke's account describes Simeon as upright or just, devout or pious, having the Spirit resting upon him, and being guided by the Spirit.

Most importantly, Simeon was *looking forward to the consolation of Israel.(Luke 2:25)* Like Zechariah previously (Luke 1:68, 78), Simeon thanks God for visiting and redeeming his people. Like Anna afterwards, Simeon was *looking for the redemption of Jerusalem.(Luke 2:38)* The trio's expectations recall the words of Isaiah of Babylon: *Comfort, O comfort my people, says your God. Speak tenderly to Jerusalem* and *The LORD has comforted his people, he has redeemed Jerusalem (Isaiah 40:1-2a ; 52:9)*

Simeon is aware that God keeps his promises. God is the source of life's good things which are summed up in the coming of the Messiah. Simon sings, *Master, now you are dismissing your servant in peace, according to your word.* He addresses God as *Master* and calls himself *servant*. The Master is setting his slave free to depart this life *in peace*. This is happening *now*. Simeon tells the Master that it is all *according to your word*. The time has come when God is keeping his promises.

Simeon is also conscious that God gives believers insight and deliverance. God is the guide of all who trust and obey the Messiah. Simeon continues to sing, *For my eyes have seen your salvation.* Simeon was the one to whom the Holy Spirit had revealed that he would not experience death until he saw the Lord's Messiah (Luke 2:26). He is seeing before his own eyes the saving power of God in the birth of the Messiah. One thinks of the stirring words of Julia Ward Howe's hymn: 'Mine eyes have seen the glory of the coming of the Lord ... His truth is marching on.'

Finally, Simeon is aware that God includes the particular and the universal in his grand plan. God is the goal of both Jews and Gentiles who follow Jesus the Messiah and the Lord. Simeon concludes by describing the salvation *which you have prepared in the presence of all peoples.*

The plural *peoples* reflects the words of Isaiah of Babylon: *The Lord shall reveal his holy arm in the sight of all the nations. (Isaiah 52:10 Greek) Peoples* in Simeon's song interprets *nations* in Isaiah's prophecy to show that God's salvation includes Jews and Gentiles.

Simeon's song mentions *a light* parallel to *your salvation.* Isaiah 49:6 speaks of Israel as *a light to the nations* and John 8:12 refers to Jesus as *the light of the world.* Simeon's words *for revelation to the Gentiles and for glory to your people Israel* underline the worldwide extent of salvation to Gentiles and the local origin of salvation from Jews.

Conclusion

At the end of a profound section of his greatest letter the apostle Paul also saw the big picture of salvation: *For from him and through him and to him are all things. To him be the glory forever. Amen.(Romans 11:36)* The New English Bible paraphrased Paul's praise brilliantly: *Source, Guide, and Goal of all that is - to him be glory for ever! Amen.*

A Kentucky farmer, who was also a deacon in his local Baptist church, used to offer a prayer which echoes Simeon's song and Paul's praise. He would say, 'O God, help us to remember where we have come from, how much we've got to do, and how much we need one another to do it. Amen.'

John the Theologian Patmos

13 The Word

Who is the Word? He is ultimately related to the Creator and the created order. In the world he experienced negative and positive responses. The Word became a human being and dwelt among us. Most importantly, believers saw his glory and received his grace. His name is Jesus Christ. He is the one in whom God comes to us and the one through whom we go to God.

Introduction

We shall understand the song at the beginning of John's Gospel better when we seek answers to two questions. First, where did the ideas in the song come from? Second, where do the ideas in the song lead to?

First, the song at the beginning of John's Gospel is about the Word. Ideas in the song come from Wisdom literature in the Old Testament and the Apocrypha.

Some examples may be noted. Behind the opening words, *In the beginning was the Word, and the Word was with God*, are the proverbial sayings: *The Lord created me (Wisdom) at the beginning of his work, the first of his acts of long ago ... I was beside him, like a master worker.(Proverbs 8:22, 30)*

Then the statements about *life, light, darkness, children of God,* and *glory* recall the apocryphal sayings: *She (Wisdom) is ... a pure emanation of the glory of the Almighty ... She is a reflection of eternal light ... She passes into holy souls and makes them friends of God ... Compared with the light she is found to be superior, for it is succeeded by the night, but against wisdom evil does not prevail.(Wisdom 7:25b, 26a, 27b, 29b, 30)*

Finally, the apocryphal writer identified Wisdom with the Law of Moses: *My Creator chose the place for my tent. He said, 'Make your dwelling in Jacob.'(Sirach 24:8b)*

John's song identifies Wisdom with Jesus the Word. Law for readers of Hebrew and Wisdom for speakers of Greek are fulfilled in the embodied Word who pitched his tent among us and revealed the glory of God.

Second, after the song there are signs of Jesus in John chapters 2 to 12 and sufferings by Jesus in John chapters 13 to 20. Ideas in the song lead to the story of Jesus including his signs and his sufferings.

The song says, *In him was life*; Jesus says, *I am the way, and the truth, and the life.(John 14:6)* The song says, *The life was the light of all people*; Jesus says, *I am the light of the world. Whoever follows me will never walk in darkness but will have the light of life.(John 8:12)*

The song says, *To all who received him ... he gave power to become children of God, who were born ... of God*; Jesus says, *Very truly, I tell you, no one can see the kingdom of God without being born from above.(John 3:3)*

And the phrase, *the glory as of the Father's only Son*, is paralleled in the famous statement, *God so loved the world that he gave his only Son.(John 3:16)*

Instead of leaving Wisdom in the realm of past ideas, the song identifies Wisdom at work in the signs and sufferings of Jesus the Word. John's Gospel must be read in the light of the song about the Word. Then the reader knows where Jesus has come from and where he is going to.

The Word and the Universe
In the beginning was the Word,
and the Word was with God,
and the Word was God.
He was in the beginning with God.
All things came into being through him,
and without him not one thing came into being.
What has come into being in him was life,
and the life was the light of all people.
The light shines in the darkness,
and the darkness did not overcome it.
(John 1:1-5)

The Word is related to the Creator. The opening words of the song echo the opening words of the Bible, *In the beginning God created the heavens and the earth. (Genesis 1:1)*

J B Phillips, the prince of paraphrasers, rendered the first lines of the song as follows: *At the beginning God expressed himself. That personal expression, that word, was with God, and was God, and he existed with God from the beginning.*

Robert Bratcher's first edition of Today's English Version also gave a fine paraphrase: *From the very beginning, when God was, the Word also was; where God was, the Word was with him; what God was, the Word also was.* By communicating the meaning of the New Testament Greek accurately both Phillips and Bratcher avoided the ancient heresy of Arius and the modern heresy of the Jehovah's Witnesses.

The Word is also related to the Creation. The Word is deliberately linked to the created order three times. Everything was made *through him*, not a single thing was made *without him*, and whatever has come to be finds true life *in him*.

The Jew would recall the teaching of Genesis 1 that God spoke his mighty word and things came to be. The Greek would think of the impersonal philosophical principle, the Logos, which Heraclitus identified as the order of creation. The Christian would know the life and teaching of Jesus and his followers that the Creator had come as the Redeemer. The message of the song to Jew, Greek, and Christian is that the created order is being restored to its intended glory by the Word.

The Word is associated with *life*, 37 times in John, and *light*, 22 times in John. The Word as God's agent of creation is not responsible for the existence of the opposites of life and light, namely, death and darkness. However, as God's agent of recreation, the Word as life and light confronts death and darkness. The Word's gifts are available to *all people*.

The good news is loud and clear: *The light shines in the darkness, and the darkness did not overcome it.* The verb translated *overcome* can mean 'to grasp with the mind' (comprehend) or 'to grasp with the hand' (overcome). The present *shines* contrasts with the past *did not overcome*. The light shines on and the darkness is as good as beaten. The darkness has neither comprehended nor conquered the light. Indeed, the darkness did not, does not, and will not master the light!

The Word and the World
> *The true light, which enlightens everyone,*
> *was coming into the world.*
> *He was in the world,*
> *and the world came into being through him;*
> *yet the world did not know him.*
> *He came to what was his own,*
> *and his own people did not accept him.*
> *But to all who received him,*
> *who believed in his name,*
> *he gave power to become children of God,*
> *who were born, not of blood*
> *or of the will of the flesh*
> *or of the will of man,*
> *but of God.*
> *(John 1:9-13)*

The song about the Word goes on to say that *the true light* was coming into the world. *The light of the world (John 8:12)* continues to shed light on everyone. The Word was in the world but there were two responses.

On the one hand, there was a negative response to the Word. The world, which came into being through the Word, did not recognise him. The Word came to *what was his own*, his own domain, but, tragically, *his own people* did not take him to themselves. The first major part of the Gospel is covered by this negative response: *He came to what was his own, and his own people did not accept him.* John chapters 2 to 12 tell of signs done by Jesus in his ministry and seen by people without insight.

On the other hand, there was a positive response. The Word gave powerful permission to as many as took him to themselves, who entrusted themselves to him, to become God's children. The second major part of the Gospel is covered by this positive response: *To all who received him, who believed in his name, he gave power to become children of God.* John chapters 13 to 20 tell of the sufferings by Jesus in his last days and seen by people with insight.

Believers were not born of *blood* (literally 'bloods' - of birth initiated by the mixing of blood of mother and father according to ancient biology), *the will of the flesh* (of birth initiated by sexual desire), *the will of man* (of birth initiated by the family patriarch).

Becoming a child of God is not a natural process but a spiritual gift. It is not a matter of belonging to a particular human family or nation but a matter of receiving the Word, believing in his name, and being given power to become a child of God. Becoming a Christian is not a matter of biology but of theology!

The song about the Word agrees with the statement of Jesus to Nicodemus, *Very truly, I tell you, no one can see the kingdom of God without being born from above.(John 3:3)*

The Word and the Community of Faith
And the Word became flesh
and lived among us,
and we have seen his glory,
the glory as of the Father's only Son,
full of grace and truth.
From his fullness we have all received,
grace upon grace.
The law indeed was given through Moses;
grace and truth came through Jesus Christ.
No one has ever seen God.
It is God the only Son, who is close to the Father's heart,
who has made him known.
(John 1:14, 16-18)

The song about the Word refers to the presence of the eternal one in time and space. The Word became *flesh*, a human being of flesh and blood, and took up his abode among men and women. The infinitive of the verb translated *lived* literally means 'to pitch a tent' or 'to dwell in a tent'.

There may be a backward glance to the tabernacle where God dwelt among Israel in the wilderness wandering (Exodus 25:8-9) and to the ideal temple after the return from exile where God will reside (Ezekiel 43:7). There may also be a forward look to the new Jerusalem where God will dwell among his people (Revelation 21:3-4). If so, the Word replaces the ancient tabernacle and foreshadows the divine presence in the last days.

The Word is glorious. In the Old Testament *glory* is associated with the tabernacle (Exodus 40:34), the temple (1 Kings 8:11), and the vision of a restored temple (Ezekiel 44:4). The implicit promise of *glory* may be explicitly fulfilled in the life of the Word. On the mount of transfiguration three disciples are said to have seen the *glory* of Jesus (Luke 9:32). Just as the song about the Word speaks of *his glory, the glory as of the Father's only Son*, so does God acknowledge Jesus as his beloved or chosen son at the transfiguration (Matthew 17:5; Mark 9:7; Luke 9:35).

> In John 1:14 I have followed the NRSV marginal reading: *the glory as of the Father's only Son.* 'The glory of a unique Son coming from the Father' points forward to such statements as *God so loved the world that he gave his only Son. (John 3:16)*

The song now picks up some catchwords. The adjective *full* is taken up by the noun *fullness*. The first of the couplet *grace and truth* is repeated twice in the phrase *grace upon grace*. The Word who is the Son has a rich fullness. He is *full of grace and truth*. Out of this fullness he gives *grace upon grace* to the community of faith.

In the Old Testament God is characterised as *abounding in steadfast love and faithfulness.(Exodus 34:6)* God's *steadfast love* is his kindness or mercy in choosing his ancient people and expressing his love in the covenant. God's *faithfulness* is his fidelity to the promises of the covenant.

In the New Testament divine reality is likewise revealed in God's Son who is *full of grace and truth*. The word *grace* only appears here in John's Gospel but is common in Luke, Acts, and Paul.

The gift of *grace upon grace* is worthy of note. It may be translated 'one favour in place of another'. In other words, the community of faith has received a succession of favours out of the rich fullness of the Word who is the Son. The song has moved from a general reference about the Word dwelling among human beings: *the Word ... lived among us.*

The song makes particular references to the glory of the Word being seen by believers and a succession of favours being received by believers from the Word: *we have seen his glory* and out of *his fullness we have all received, grace upon grace.*

Finally, the song about the Word reveals the name of the one who surpasses even Moses. Moses had been the mediator of *the law* in which God revealed himself at Sinai and Moses was the chief character in the first five books of the Hebrew Bible.

Beyond the promise made by God in Moses comes the promise kept by God through *Jesus Christ*. The divine reality of *grace and truth* is seen and made known in *God the only Son, who is close to the Father's heart*. The end of the song brings us back to the beginning: the Word with God.

Conclusion
When Aurelius Augustine was 32 years old, he was a professor of rhetoric at the University of Milan. He had searched for truth in the books of Platonist philosophers. He had found similar ideas in both John's Gospel and the Platonists, such as the existence of the Word in the beginning, the identity of the Word with God, the creative power of the Word, the revealing of truth by the Word. But Augustine had not found in his Greek

philosophy the following ideas about the Word: *But to all who received him, who believed in his name, he gave power to become children of God, who were born ... of God. And the Word became flesh and lived among us, and we have seen his glory, the glory as of a father's only son, full of grace and truth.* This quotation marked the difference between his Greek philosophy and the Christian faith.

In 386 Augustine was still living a life of pleasure but he was not happy. One day he was sitting in the garden of his home. He heard a child's voice calling out in Latin, 'Tolle, lege! Tolle, lege!' (Take up and read! Take up and read!) He picked up a copy of Paul's letters and read these words: *Let us live honourably as in the day, not in revelling and drunkenness, not in debauchery and licentiousness, not in quarrelling and jealousy.* He had done all of these things. He continued reading: *Instead, put on the Lord Jesus Christ, and make no provision for the flesh, to gratify its desires.(Romans 13:13-14)*

After reading this passage, Augustine said, 'No further would I read, nor had I any need; instantly, at the end of this sentence, a clear light flooded my heart and all the darkness of doubt vanished away.'

He received and believed in the Word whose name is Jesus Christ. He was given the power to become a child of God. He saw the glory of a unique Son coming from the Father. As a member of the community of faith Augustine received a succession of favours out of the rich fullness of the Word who is the Son. He went on to be a leading thinker of Western Christianity. His writings became the foundation of European scholarship for more than a thousand years.

14 The Mind of Christ

The song in Philippians 2:5-11 encourages us to follow Christ's example. Instead of imagining that equality with God meant **getting**, Jesus knew that it meant **giving**. He gave by emptying himself and taking the form of a slave. He gave by humbling himself and becoming obedient to the point of death.

Introduction

Philippians is a letter in which Paul shows real joy as part of true friendship towards his Christian brothers and sisters in the Roman colony of Philippi. He makes a plea for Christian identity based on the example of Christ in a song about the Mind of Christ. This song covers three stages in the good news of Jesus the Messiah and the Lord.

The Pre-existent Christ

> *Let the same mind be in you that was in Christ Jesus,*
> *who, though he was in the form of God,*
> *did not regard equality with God*
> *as something to be exploited,*
> *but emptied himself,*
> *taking the form of a slave.*
> *(Philippians 2:5-7a)*

Paul introduces the song with a command in Greek which reads literally, 'Think this among you which also in Christ Jesus.'

On the one hand, the reference can be to the past: *Let the same mind be in you that was in Christ Jesus.* The readers are urged to adopt the same attitude which was also found in the Messiah. Christians are to follow the example of Jesus. On the other hand, the reference can be to the present: *Let the same mind be in you that you have in Christ Jesus.(NRSV margin)* In accord with Philippians 2:2, the readers are being urged to adopt the appropriate attitude for people who proclaim the saving events of Christ. Christians are to tell the message of Jesus. There are elements of truth in both interpretations. However, the following discussion will reveal my preference towards the first.

Throughout the song we find the same ideas in different words which appear in parallel lines. In this part of the song *the form of God* means *equality with God* and *emptied himself* is the same as *taking the form of a slave*. Christ decided that his divine status was not *something to be exploited.*

The pre-existent Christ realised that being equal with God meant giving rather than getting. By worldly reckoning he might have expected to help himself to whatever he wanted, but he did not do so. Instead, he took the form of a servant and was born in human likeness.

There may be a contrast between the attitudes of Adam, in the story of Genesis, and Christ, the Second Adam. Adam became proud and tried to outdo God, whereas Christ was unselfish and took the form of a servant. This contrast is a general one. Adam does not exist before he becomes a human being in the Genesis story. Christ does pre-exist before he takes the form of a servant. The Gospel tradition includes a reference to preexistence: *Father, glorify me in your own presence with the glory that I had in your presence before the world existed.(John 17:5)*

There may be an echo of the Suffering Servant in Isaiah 53. Christ *emptied himself, taking the form of a slave.* We shall return to this possibility in the song. The Gospel tradition does include the famous reference to being a servant: *the Son of Man came not to be served but to serve, and to give his life a ransom for many.(Mark 10:45)*

The Earthly Jesus

> *Being born in human likeness.*
> *And being found in human form,*
> *he humbled himself*
> *and became obedient to the point of death*
> *—even death on a cross.*
> *(Philippians 2:7b-8)*

As we have noted, throughout the song we find the same ideas in different words which appear in parallel lines. In this part of the song *human likeness* means *human form* and *humbled himself* is the same as *became obedient. The point of death* is explained intensively as *even death on a cross.*

The earthly Jesus realised that being equal with God meant giving rather than getting. The self-emptying of Christ is expressed in true humiliation and real obedience of the earthly Jesus who suffered death on a cross. Indeed, this part of the song ends with a punchline: *even death on a cross.*

The contrast between Adam and Christ is continued. In the Genesis story Adam's death results from disobedience but in the Gospel account Christ's death is a consequence of obedience. Elsewhere Paul spelled out the contrast: *"The first man, Adam, became a living being"; the last Adam became a life-giving spirit ... The first man was from the earth, a man of dust; the second man is from heaven.(1 Corinthians 15:45, 47)*

A further echo of the Suffering Servant may be found in Christ's humility and obedience to death: *he poured out himself to death.(Isaiah 53:12)* This is in tune with the song's message that being equal with God means giving not getting.

The Risen Lord

> ***Therefore God also highly exalted him***
> ***and gave him the name***
> ***that is above every name,***
> ***so that at the name of Jesus***
> ***every knee should bend,***
> ***in heaven and on earth and under the earth,***
> ***and every tongue should confess***
> ***that Jesus Christ is Lord,***
> ***to the glory of God the Father.***
> ***(Philippians 2:9-11)***

To the very end of the song we find the same ideas in different words which appear in parallel lines. In this part of the song *highly exalted* means *the name that is above every name* and *every knee should bend* is the same as *every tongue should confess*. Jesus receives the divine rank which was always from eternity his by right. The song tells us about the destiny of the risen Lord and ends with a punchline: *to the glory of God the Father.*

Paul's song is saying that because of the self-giving of Christ on the cross, God exalted him to his pre-existent great height and gave him an unparalleled name. A possible echo of the Suffering Servant is the exaltation of the crucified Christ: *See, my servant shall prosper; he shall be exalted and lifted up, and shall be very high.(Isaiah 52:13)*

One reading of the song says that the name is God's own name in the Old Testament, the Lord. If Christ is acknowledged as Lord, there would also be the countercultural denial of such a sacred name as Lord to the Roman Emperor in a Roman colony like Philippi.

Another reading of the song is that the name is Jesus, which means Saviour. Because Christ took the form of a servant and was born in human likeness, because Christ's self-emptying is expressed in true humiliation and real obedience, the human name of Jesus is acclaimed as the highest name and the man Jesus is acclaimed as Lord, *to the glory of God the Father.*

Accordingly, when the name of Jesus is spoken every power in heaven, earth, and hell should, and shall, bow in worship and every person in creation should, and shall, confess that Jesus the Messiah is Lord, the Son in whom we see the glory of the Father. The universal lordship of Christ is, and will be, the fulfilment of the words of the God of Isaiah of Babylon, *To me every knee shall bow, every tongue shall swear.(Isaiah 45:23)*

Conclusion

In 1850 a 15 year old English boy was feeling forsaken and forlorn when he found shelter in a Methodist Chapel on a Sunday morning. An unknown lay preacher tried to preach on a text from Isaiah of Babylon, *Turn to me and be saved, all the ends of the earth! For I am God, and there is no other.(Isaiah 45:22)* At one stage the preacher pointed and said, 'That young man there looks very miserable. Look! Look, young man! Look now!'

Later he would write in his autobiography, 'I saw what a Saviour Christ was ... I no sooner saw whom I was to believe than I also understood what it was to believe, and I did believe in one moment. And as the snow fell on my road home from the little house of prayer I thought every snowflake talked with me and told of the pardon I had found, for I was white as the driven snow through the grace of God.'

Back home his mother looked at the youth and said, 'Something wonderful has happened to you.' Four months later, after some serious reading of the Bible, the young man was baptized by immersion in a river and joined a Baptist Church. His name was Charles Haddon Spurgeon.

When Spurgeon died at the age of 57 he had a congregation of more than 5000 in London. He had established a Pastor's College. He supported evangelistic, educational, and social agencies. Despite ill health and controversy, he remained a humble, sincere, and enthusiastic believer. His commonsense and idealism appealed to ordinary people. He embodied the features which Paul extols in such letters as Philippians.

15 The Firstborn

Almighty God and merciful Father,
we give you hearty thanks for all your goodness and loving-kindness to us and to all people.
We bless you for our **creation** and **preservation**,
and all the blessings of this life;
but above all, for your immeasurable love in the **redemption** of the world by our Lord Jesus Christ,
for the means of grace and the hope of glory.

from The General Thanksgiving

Introduction

Colossians is a letter in which Paul deals with a deviation from the truth. The false teaching appears to be a mixture of Jewish and Greek ideas, which interpreted Jesus as one among several cosmic forces.

The angelic powers, which mediated the Jewish law, may be identified with the planetary powers. In Greek thought, they share in the fullness of the divine nature and control the encounter between the heavens and the earth.

Paul's response is in the words of a sacred song. Paul's song corrects the false teachers' misunderstanding of Christ by stressing his uniqueness in our creation, preservation, and redemption.

Creation

*He is the image of the invisible God,
the firstborn of all creation;
for in him all things
in heaven and on earth were created,
things visible and invisible,
whether thrones or dominions or rulers or powers—
all things have been created through him and for him.
(Colossians 1:15-16)*

The first stanza of Paul's song reminds readers of the opening words of the Hebrew Bible: *In a beginning God created the heavens and the earth. (Genesis 1:1 Literal Translation)* The first of four meanings of the Hebrew word for 'beginning' is applied to Christ: *He is ... the **firstborn** of all creation.* This means that Christ has primacy in time and rank over all creation. It does **not** mean that Christ is the first of God's creatures as ancient Arians taught and modern Jehovah's Witnesses teach.

Paul's song also reminds readers of Wisdom (Sophia) in the Greek Old Testament and Apocrypha: *For she* (Wisdom) *is ... an image of his* (God's) *goodness.(Wisdom 7:26c) The Lord created me* (Wisdom) *at the beginning of his work, the first of his acts of long ago ... When he* (God) *established the heavens, I* (Wisdom) *was there ... when he marked out the foundations of the earth, then I was beside him, like a master worker. (Proverbs 8:22, 27a, 29a, 30a) I* (Wisdom) *compassed the vault of heaven and traversed the depths of the abyss. Over waves of the sea, over all the earth, and over every people and nation I have held sway.(Sirach 24:5-6)* These allusions to Wisdom explain Christ as the image of God and the one through whom God created all things.

The utilisation of Hebrew and Greek thought refutes the false interpretation of Jesus as one among several cosmic forces. To the contrary, Christ is supreme from the first to the last.

As we noted above, the ancient Arian and modern Jehovah's Witness interpretation misreads Paul. The picture of the firstborn means primacy in time and rank. The personification of Wisdom means that God is immanent in creation. The following words of the song argue that in Christ *all things in heaven and on earth were created* and that through Christ and for Christ *all things have been created*. Christ has rulership and primacy within creation and Christ is God's agent over creation. What is implicit in Paul's song about God and Christ is what is explicit in the historic creeds about the Father and the Son.

Preservation

He himself is before all things,
and in him all things hold together.
He is the head
of the body, the church.
(Colossians 1:17-18a)

The bridge of Paul's song continues to recall the opening words of the Hebrew Bible: *In a beginning God created the heavens and the earth. (Genesis 1:1 Literal Translation)* The second and third meanings of the Hebrew word for 'beginning' are applied to Christ: *In him all things **hold together** ... He is the **head** of the body*. Christ is the divine glue which keeps all things on track and his is the supremacy at work through the people of God.

Paul's song also continues to echo Word (Logos) in the Greek Old Testament and Apocrypha: *By his* (God's) *word all things hold together.(Sirach 43:26b)* By Christ, the Word of God, all things cohere.

The utilisation of Hebrew and Greek thought continues to refute the false interpretation of Jesus as one among several cosmic forces. In reality, Christ is the preexistent one who creates and sustains all things. Furthermore, Christ the creator and sustainer has supremacy over the new creation in the universal church. The universal church is seen in the local congregations who gather Sunday by Sunday to praise and worship God through Christ.

Redemption
He is the beginning,
the firstborn from the dead,
so that he might come to have first place in everything.
For in him all the fullness of God was pleased to dwell,
and through him God was pleased to reconcile to himself
all things, whether on earth or in heaven,
by making peace through the blood of his cross.
(Colossians 1:18b-20)

The second stanza of Paul's song includes a reminder of the opening words of Genesis twice. The fourth and first meanings of the Hebrew word for 'beginning' are applied to Christ: *He is the* ***beginning,*** the ***firstborn*** *from the dead*. Christ is the new start for God's people. By his resurrection Christ is supreme over all.

Paul's song also includes another echo of Wisdom (Sophia) in the Greek Old Testament: *The Lord created me* (Wisdom) *at the beginning of his work, the first of his acts of long ago. (Proverbs 8: 22)* As Wisdom is the beginning of God's ways, so is Christ in the beginning of God's new ways.

The utilisation of Hebrew and Greek thought concludes the rebuttal of the false interpretation of Jesus as one among several cosmic forces. Paul teaches his readers to appreciate Jesus as Christ over all in creation, preservation, and, most emphatically, redemption.

The song goes beyond its predecessors in a notable fashion. There has been a major disruption in God's old creation which leads to a marvellous development in God's new creation. Christ is not only the divine agent in creation but he is also the divine agent in new creation. He is the cosmic Christ in whom *all the fullness of God was pleased to dwell*. He is the crucified Christ; *through him God was pleased to reconcile to himself all things*. He is the risen Lord who is *the firstborn from the dead, so that he might come to have first place in everything.*

Paul's song speaks of the cosmic Christ, the one in whom *all the fullness of God was pleased to dwell*. Paul's letter later says, *In him the whole fullness of deity dwells bodily. (Colossians 2:9)* The work of God and Christ is fully and wholly unified. Christ is uniquely related to God personally. Christ has a unique role in God's work. Yet there is a distinction within the unity. Christ is *both* as Beginning and Wisdom to be identified with God the creator and the redeemer *and* as the Son to be distinguished from the Father.

Paul's song also speaks of the crucified Christ, the one through whom *God was pleased to reconcile to himself all things*.

Christ did this *by making peace through the blood of his cross.* Christ shed his blood in sacrifice. Paul speaks of *redemption that is in Christ Jesus, whom God put forward as a sacrifice of atonement by his blood, effective through faith. (Romans 3:25)* He died a criminal's death on a Roman cross. As Paul says, *he humbled himself and became obedient to the point of death—even death on a cross.(Philippians 2:8)* Christ completes and gives meaning to creation alienated from the creator in the reconciliation effected by his victory over evil and death. As Paul says, *In Christ God was reconciling the world to himself. (2 Corinthians 5:19)*

Finally, Paul's song speaks of the risen Lord. The resurrection parallels the creation. Christ is *the firstborn from the dead* as Christ is *the firstborn of all creation.* Christ is the one through whom all things were made, the one in whom all things cohere, the one by whom all created things are reconciled to the Creator and to his other creatures.

Conclusion

Paul has reminded us of who Christ is and what Christ does in creation, preservation, and redemption:

The first stanza of the song says that Jesus Christ is Lord of the universe. God has acted with cosmic significance in Christ who is **the Source** of all that exists.

The bridge of the song says that Jesus Christ is before all things in time and rank. Christ is **the Guide** of all in creation and new creation.

The second stanza of the song says that Jesus Christ is Lord of the church. Christ is everything the Christian needs. He reveals God to us and restores us to God. Christ is **the Goal** of all that exists.

16 The Son

According to the unknown author of the Letter to the Hebrews, Jesus is God's last word, heir of all things, maker of the universe, the reflection of God's glory, the very image of God's essence, the upholder of all things, the purifier for our sins, and the one enthroned at God's right hand.

Long ago God spoke to our ancestors in many and various ways by the prophets,
but in these last days he has spoken to us by a Son,
whom he appointed heir of all things,
through whom he also created the worlds.
He is the reflection of God's glory
and the exact imprint of God's very being,
and he sustains all things by his powerful word.
When he had made purification for sins,
he sat down at the right hand of the Majesty on high,
having become as much superior to angels
as the name he has inherited is more excellent than theirs.
(Hebrews 1:1-4)

Introduction
At the beginning of the so called Letter to the Hebrews is a truly memorable song about Jesus Christ. The book may well be a collection of sermons. It would be most appropriate for the unknown preacher to commence with this superb poetry in a book which spells out the wonder of his subject: *Jesus Christ is the same yesterday and today and forever.(Hebrews 13:8)*

God Has Spoken

First, it is true to say that the Old Testament is God's promise *in many and various ways*. There are narratives of beginnings, ancestors, refugees, invaders, kings, prophets, exiles, returnees, and rebels. There are also contributions of worshippers, sages, and storytellers. All of them sought to worship and understand God, to trust and obey God in many times and various places. They all looked forward to something better, someone better.

Second, it is also true to say that the New Testament is God's fulfilment in one person: *in these last days he has spoken to us by a Son.* The Letter to the Hebrews has many allusions to and major citations of the Old Testament to explain the significance of Jesus Christ. It appears to be written to Christians who are attracted to return to Jewish ways. With an intricate argument, the author of Hebrews confronts the possible heresy of leaving the truth of Jesus for the error of not appreciating all that Jesus has done. The age of promise has led to the age of fulfilment.

In the clause, *having become as much superior to angels*, the word translated *superior* is literally the comparative adjective 'better'. It actually occurs 13 times in Hebrews (1:4; 6:9; 7:7, 19, 22; 8:6 (twice); 9:23; 10:34; 11:16, 35, 40; 12:24). Among the better things are a hope, a covenant, promises, sacrifices, a country, a resurrection, a word. The Old Testament promise was good, the New Testament fulfilment is better.

God's Last Word

God's last word is One who is Son. The song at the beginning of Hebrews describes him in seven ways:
    God appointed him heir of all things.
    Through him God made the worlds.

He is the reflection of God's glory.
He is the very image of the essence of God.
He upholds all things by his powerful word.
He made purification for our sins.
He is enthroned at the right hand of God.
Therefore, he is better than the angels and has inherited a more distinguished title than theirs.

First, the song deals with God's relation to the Son. To see One who is Son is to see God who is Father. According to the Fourth Gospel Jesus said, *Whoever has seen me has seen the Father.(John 14:9)* Accordingly, Hebrews says that God appointed the Son *heir of all things* and through the Son God *created the worlds.*

On the one hand, *heir of all things* recalls a royal psalm which came to be interpreted messianically. God's anointed king is referred to as God's son and he inherits the nations: *You are my son; today I have begotten you. Ask of me, and I will make the nations your heritage, and the ends of the earth your possession. (Psalm 2:7-8)*

On the other hand, the idea of being the one *through whom he also created the worlds* parallels concepts in John 1:3 and Colossians 1:16 which make allusions to Wisdom as the one through whom God created all things.

Second, the song deals with the Son's relation to God. He is the radiance or *reflection of God's glory*. He radiates or reflects the glory of God just as the rays of the sun give light and heat to the earth. He is the stamp or *exact imprint of God's very being*. He shows us exactly what God is like just as a seal makes an impression in wax on a legal document. Humanly speaking, we sometimes say that someone is a chip off the old block.

Hebrews uses the language of the apocryphal book of Wisdom to explain the Son: Wisdom *is a breath of the power of God, and a pure emanation of the glory of the Almighty ... a reflection of eternal light, a spotless mirror of the working of God, and an image of his goodness.(Wisdom 7:25-26)*

The Son is also the one who *sustains all things by his powerful word*. Hebrews parallels the idea in Paul that *in him* (Christ) *all things hold together.(Colossians 1:17)*

Finally, the Son is also the priest who *made purification for sins* and the king who *sat down at the right hand of the Majesty on high*. The figures of priest and king are developed in Hebrews to explain the person and work of Christ.

For example, it is said, *Since, then, we have a great high priest who has passed through the heavens, Jesus, the Son of God, let us hold fast to our confession.(Hebrews 4:14)* It is also said, *Now the main point in what we are saying is this: we have such a high priest, one who is seated at the right hand of the throne of the Majesty in the heavens. (Hebrews 8:1)*

In fact, the extended argument of Hebrews utilises two figures from another royal psalm which came to be interpreted of the Messiah: *The LORD says to my lord, "Sit at my right hand until I make your enemies your footstool." The LORD has sworn and will not change his mind, "You are a priest forever according to the order of Melchizedek."(Psalm 110:1, 4)*

The Protestant Reformers developed the ideas of Jesus as prophet, priest, and king. The seeds of these ideas are in Hebrews. Jesus is the prophet through whom God has spoken his last word. Jesus is the priest who has made purification for our sins. Jesus is the king who has sat down at the place of honour alongside God in heaven.

Yes, says Hebrews, the Son is better than the angels. Yes, his title is more distinguished than theirs. And who is the Son? Hebrews doesn't name him for a while. Then we read about him: *We do see Jesus, who for a little while was made lower than the angels, now crowned with glory and honour because of the suffering of death, so that by the grace of God he might taste death for everyone.(Hebrews 2:9)*

Later on we note that he is not just a personification of Wisdom but a real person: *In the days of his flesh, Jesus offered up prayers and supplications ... Although he was a Son, he learned obedience through what he suffered.(Hebrews 5:7-8)* Indeed, readers are given the stirring exhortation: *Let us run with perseverance the race that is set before us, looking to Jesus the pioneer and perfecter of our faith.(Hebrews 12:1b-2a)*

Conclusion

In his autobiography *Oh God, What Next?* Hugh Montefiore tells how he changed from being a Jew to becoming a Christian. He was 16 years of age. As he sat alone in his study at Rugby School on a wintry afternoon during 1936, he had a totally unexpected and most unusual experience. All of a sudden in his mind's eye he became aware of a figure in white. He heard the words 'Follow me'.

Hugh had become aware of Jesus the living Christ and therefore he had become aware of God in a new way. At the time he knew nothing about the Christian Church and very little of Christianity. But he had been converted by a vision of Jesus, not a vision of the Church.

Montefiore's career as a pastor, a lecturer, and a writer included a commentary on the Letter to the Hebrews. This was quite fitting for someone who had a vision of Jesus and heard the voice of Jesus. The Letter encourages us to be people who are *looking to Jesus the pioneer and perfecter of our faith. (Hebrews 12:2a)* Montefiore himself translated these words as 'keeping our eyes on him who inspires our faith from the beginning to the end, Jesus'.

When we have our eyes fixed on Jesus we hear the words 'Follow me'. In his famous book, *The Quest of the Historical Jesus*, Albert Schweitzer echoed these words of Jesus to Peter in Mark 1 and John 21: 'He (Jesus) comes to us as One unknown, without a name, as of old, by the lake-side, He came to those men who knew Him not. He speaks to us the same word: "Follow thou me!" and sets us to the tasks which He has to fulfil for our time. He commands. And to those who obey Him, whether they be wise or simple, He will reveal himself in the toils, the conflicts, the sufferings which they must pass through in His fellowship and, as an ineffable mystery, they shall learn in their own experience Who He is.'

17 The Lord and the Lamb

Five songs in Revelation 4 and 5 reminded the original readers and listeners that heaven is near for those with eyes to see. In God's good time they would be assured that the will of the Lord and the Lamb shall be done on earth as in heaven. The heavenly songs provide the perspective of faith for the sufferings of earth.

Introduction
The last book in the Bible is called Revelation, a Latin word, or Apocalypse, a Greek word. It is a representative of revelatory or apocalyptic literature and includes strange symbols and secret codes. Such literature was written in times of crisis. Towards the end of the first century followers of Jesus faced the possibility of persecution or martyrdom, the peril of compromise with idolatrous and unjust culture, and the uncertainty of political and religious chaos.

In these turbulent times John the prophet of Patmos sends forth the message of God's final victory over the powers of evil and death to believers in seven congregations of God's people in the Roman province of Asia.

As he does so, he tells of his vision of God and Christ who are actually in the control room of the universe at the heavenly headquarters. The vision in Revelation 4 and 5 sets the scene for the rest of the book.

After the series of seals, trumpets, and bowls John will visualise the defeat of the powers of evil and death and the victory of God and Christ. Revelation 21 and 22 describe a new heaven and a new earth, and the new holy city, of which it is said: *Its temple is the Lord God the Almighty and the Lamb ... and its lamp is the Lamb ... the throne of God and of the Lamb will be in it.(Revelation 21:22, 23; 22:3)*

The original readers of and listeners to the drama which is the book of Revelation could join in the worship of the heavenly throng despite the earthly confusion surrounding them. God the creator in Revelation 4 is God the redeemer in Revelation 5.

The Almighty
Holy, holy, holy,
the Lord God the Almighty,
who was and is and is to come.
(Revelation 4:8)

The singers are the four living creatures. They are like the guardians of God's throne in Ezekiel 1. In Revelation 4 and 5 they represent the whole created order. They signify what is noblest - **a lion**, what is strongest - **an ox**, what is wisest - **a human being**, and what is swiftest - **an eagle**, in nature.

The words *Holy, holy, holy* recall Isaiah's vision of God in the temple in which seraphs say, *Holy, holy, holy is the LORD of hosts; the whole earth is full of his glory.(Isaiah 6:3)* However, John's vision focusses not on the creation but the creator. In addition to holiness, *Holy, holy, holy,* God's nature includes omnipotence, *the Almighty*, and eternity, *who was and is and is to come.*

God's **holiness** means that he is set apart from evil and injustice. God's **omnipotence** is conveyed in the Greek words translated *the Lord God the Almighty*. The word *Almighty* is used in the Greek Old Testament to translate two Hebrew names for God: 'LORD of Hosts' (YHWH Sebaoth) and 'God Almighty' (El Shaddai). God's **eternity** is spelled out in ungrammatical Greek which may be translated literally, 'the was and the being and the coming'.

It has been suggested that the author of Revelation thinks in Hebrew but writes in Greek. Indeed, *who was and is and is to come* could be a new explanation of YHWH, God's name in the Hebrew Old Testament, which has been traditionally translated 'LORD'. Interestingly, James Moffatt translated the divine name in the Old Testament as 'the Eternal'.

John, the prophet of Patmos, by recording the song of the four living creatures is announcing that the holy and almighty God of the Christians was, and is, and ever shall be. Down through the years Christians have drawn strength from John's vision and have joined the whole created order in singing the praises of the almighty God.

The Creator
   You are worthy, our Lord and God,
   to receive glory and honour and power,
   for you created all things,
   and by your will they existed and were created.
   (Revelation 4:11)

The song is sung by the twenty-four elders who represent the twelve tribes of Israel and the twelve disciples of Jesus. In other words, the people of God under the old and new covenants fall down in worship before the enthroned creator and sustainer of all the universe.

As we shall see, not only is the creator in Revelation 4 *worthy ... to receive glory and honour and power* so also is the redeemer in Revelation 5. The word *worthy* is related to the idea of fitness. The creating God is more than qualified to receive the acknowledgement of his creation. To God belong *glory and honour and power*, a divine trio of splendour, reverence, energy.

God the creator is addressed as *worthy* of *glory and honour and power* for two reasons. It is because he created everything - *for you created all things*. It is also because everything came into existence for the sake of his good intention - *for the sake of* (rather than *by*) *your will they existed and were created.* Despite the creation's confusion and chaos, God intended to bring all things into harmony with him from the very beginning.

The message of the Patmos prophet in Revelation 21 and 22 is that the first heaven and the first earth afflicted by the mysterious powers of evil and death will finally achieve the divine purpose with the coming of the new heaven and the new earth. As we shall see, this is because God the creator in Revelation 4 is also God the redeemer in Revelation 5.

When John recorded his visions Domitian was the Roman Emperor. He was issuing edicts with the words, 'Our Lord and God commands', and was requiring from his citizens the greeting, 'Hail to the Lord of Lords!' John, the prophet of

Patmos, by recording the song of the twenty-four elders is announcing that the true Lord and God is the one and only creator. Since then Christians have been encouraged by this vision and have joined the whole people of God in singing the praises of the creating God.

The Redeemer
> *You are worthy to take the scroll*
> *and to open its seals,*
> *for you were slaughtered and by your blood*
> *you ransomed for God saints*
> *from every tribe and language and people and nation;*
> *you have made them to be a kingdom and priests*
> *serving our God,*
> *and they will reign on earth.*
> *(Revelation 5:9-10)*

The singers are the four living creatures, the noblest, strongest, wisest, and swiftest in nature, and the twenty-four elders, the people of God under the old and new covenants. The song is sung to the Lamb who shares the worth and the worship of God.

The Lamb is portrayed as having seven horns, a symbol of strength, and seven eyes, a symbol of knowledge. The horns and the eyes are the seven spirits, a symbol of God's Spirit. In other words, the Spirit of God is sent into the world as the strength and knowledge of the Lamb.

The Lamb is identified as *the Lion of the tribe of Judah* and *the Root of David.(Revelation 5:5)* Some Old Testament background is helpful. *The Lion* recalls a blessing in Genesis which was interpreted messianically: *Judah is a lion's whelp ... The sceptre shall not depart from Judah ... (Genesis 49:9-10)* **The Root** is reminiscent of a prophecy in Isaiah which was interpreted messianically: *A shoot shall come out from the stump of Jesse, and a branch shall grow out of his roots. (Isaiah 11:1)*

The victorious Lion also known as the slaughtered Lamb is considered worthy because he is able to open the seals of the scroll of God's redemptive plan for the destiny of the world.

The Lamb is an image of sacrifice. Biblical associations include the divine command for Abraham to sacrifice his only son Isaac (Genesis 22), the directions for the people of Israel to sacrifice the Passover Lamb (Exodus 12), and the provision of the Suffering Servant, like a lamb that is led to the slaughter, who poured out himself to death and bore the sin of many (Isaiah 53).

The most important association of the image is the death of Jesus on the cross. The Fourth Gospel records the memorable words of John the Baptist: *Here is the Lamb of God who takes away the sin of the world!(John 1:29)* An unsolved puzzle of the New Testament is the use of the same symbol but different Greek words for *Lamb* in John 1 and Revelation 5.

A new Passover could be indicated by the reference to the *slaughtered* Lamb's *blood* and a new Exodus could be indicated by the reference to being *ransomed for God* and being made *a kingdom and priests.* Israel's liberation from Egypt was intended to produce *a priestly kingdom and a holy nation.(Exodus 19:6)*

Unlike the first Passover and Exodus which related to members of twelve tribes, the new Passover and Exodus encompass believers from *every tribe and language and people and nation.*

The followers of Christ are both *a kingdom and priests.* Christ has inaugurated the kingdom of God in his victorious life and death. Christ's triumph over evil and death has begun the divine process of transformation and renewal. Christ has given himself in sacrificial obedience to the point of death on the cross. Christ is the priestly figure who comes to us from God and goes from us to God.

Christians share his royal authority over the whole creation and his priestly work in the worldwide mission and ministry of the church. If we live out our destiny as believers sent by God to our needy world, and if we truly embody the beliefs and practices of Jesus the Lord in our everyday life, then we are *a kingdom and priests serving* (literally, *to*) *our God, who will reign on earth*, when God's will shall be done on earth as in heaven.

The Lamb
Worthy is the Lamb that was slaughtered
to receive power and wealth and wisdom
and might and honour and glory and blessing!
(Revelation 5:12)

In addition to the four living creatures of earth, and the twenty-four elders of time before and after Christ, the song is sung by the countless angels of heaven to the Lamb.

Just as the creating God was accounted *worthy* of worship and receives *glory and honour and power* in Revelation 4, the redeeming Lamb in Revelation 5 is accounted *worthy* of worship and receives *glory and honour and power*.

The worship offered to God the Lord is to the Creator who has plans for his creation and the worship offered to Christ the Lamb is to the Redeemer who accomplishes the plans of his Father. His redemptive death is emphasised by the reference to being *slaughtered*.

Altogether seven attributes are ascribed to the Lamb: *power and wealth and wisdom and might and honour and glory and blessing!* It is truly a paradox that a man who died a criminal's death in an obscure corner of a mighty empire is treated as a crucified conqueror!

The paradox of the Crucified God is apparent in the rest of the New Testament.

> To his listeners Jesus said, *If any want to become my followers, let them deny themselves and take up their cross and follow me. (Mark 8:34)*

> At the place of crucifixion the Roman Governor *had an inscription written and put on the cross. It read, "Jesus of Nazareth, the King of the Jews." (John 19:19)*

> To fellow believers Paul wrote, *The message about the cross is foolishness to those who are perishing, but to us*

who are being saved it is the power of God.(1 Corinthians 1:18)

An unknown writer urged his readers to be *looking to Jesus the pioneer and perfecter of our faith, who ... endured the cross, disregarding its shame, and has taken his seat at the right hand of the throne of God.(Hebrews 12:2)*

Peter also wrote, *He himself bore our sins in his body on the cross, so that, free from sins, we might live for righteousness; by his wounds you have been healed.(1 Peter 2:24)*

The Lord and the Lamb
To the one seated on the throne and to the Lamb
be blessing and honour and glory and might
for ever and ever!
(Revelation 5:13)

The singers are every creature in the universe from the beginning of God's creation through all time to the end of God's creation. The recipients of praise and worship are the Lord of Revelation 4 and the Lamb of Revelation 5. The Lord of creation and the Lamb of redemption share the throne at the heavenly headquarters.

In the song the whole created order ascribes to the Lord and the Lamb *blessing and honour and glory and might*. The Creator and the Redeemer are given praise, respect, splendour, and sovereignty by all people and all things. The four living creatures of the earth say, 'Amen!' The twenty-four elders of the old and new covenants fall down and worship.

Conclusion

Among notable attempts to take the message of the Lord and the Lamb to the whole world is the unexpected case of William Carey the cobbler.

The 31 year old pastor preached a sermon to a Baptist Association in Nottingham, England on May 30, 1792. The theme of his 'Deathless Sermon' was 'Expect great things from God! Attempt great things for God!' He based the sermon on a text from the Old Testament: *Enlarge the site of your tent, and let the curtains of your habitations be stretched out ...(Isaiah 54:2-3)* Carey advocated the preaching of the Gospel to the heathen in foreign lands. As a result, the next day a Baptist Missionary Society was formed.

Previously, William Carey had written and published his manifesto for missions, *An Enquiry Into The Obligations Of Christians To Use Means For The Conversion Of The Heathens* (Leicester, 1792). He challenged his readers to consider 'the religious state of the world, the success of former undertakings, and the practicality of further undertakings.'

When Carey wrote his *Enquiry* less than one in four of the world's population of 731 million was nominally Christian. He was concerned for 420 million who were 'still in pagan darkness' and 130 million who were the followers of Muhammad. He was also aware of 'a very great degree of ignorance and immorality' among Christians who numbered

100 million Catholics, 44 million Protestants, 30 million Greeks and Armenians. Finally, he mentioned 7 million Jews.

Carey advocated a missionary strategy of praying, planning, and paying. The shoemaker pastor wrote for his own denomination but without prejudice to other churches. 'There is room enough for us all, without interfering with each other ... Each denomination would bear good will to the other, and wish, and pray for its success, considering it as upon the whole friendly to the great cause of true religion.'

Subsequently, William Carey went to India. Through trials and tribulations he learned Bengali, began translating the Bible and preaching to small groups. Eventually he formed a team of two teachers and one printer. After seven years he baptized his first convert and published his Bengali New Testament. In the next 28 years Carey and his Indian helpers translated the entire Bible into India's six major languages.

He lived in India for 41 years and his converts numbered 700. He sought social reforms in India such as the abolishing the sacrifice of children, the burning of widows, and the assistance of suicide. William Carey inspired a golden age of missions in the nineteenth century.

Serampore College in West Bengal, India was founded by William Carey, Joshua Marshman, and William Ward in 1818. The trio's aim was to give an education in arts and sciences to students of every 'caste, colour or country' and to train people for ministry in the growing church in India. Like Carey, Marshman, and Ward we may be assured that the will of the Lord and the Lamb shall be done on earth as it is in heaven.

John the Seer Patmos

Postscript

Let the word of Christ dwell in you richly; teach and admonish one another in all wisdom; and with gratitude in your hearts sing psalms, hymns, and spiritual songs to God.(Colossians 3:16)

I remember my visit to the North West Indian city of Amritsar, meaning 'Lake of Amrit'. Amrit is Punjabi for 'the water of immortality'. The city is the site of the Golden Temple of the Sikhs. The Sikh founder saw himself as a bridge between Hindus and Muslims. Sikhs have a holy book, their eleventh guru, and worship their personal God.

The Golden Temple stands on pillars in the midst of a lake, 150 metres square. Pilgrims wash their feet when they arrive and, before they leave, sip the water and sprinkle their eyes. The temple is 52 metres square, has white marble lower parts, and its upper parts are covered with gilded copper plates. A causeway, 60 metres long, connects the building with a western archway. The visual effect is stunning. The personal experience, if you are a Sikh, is as real and tangible as the water of the lake. You are washed, refreshed, and enlightened.

After seeing the Golden Temple, I was told about a recent Hindu copy of the Sikh sacred site. It was built to honour Rama, son of Brahman, Krishna, the hero god, and Lakshmi, wife of Vishnu. When I asked after lunch if I could see the Hindu temple, I was told that it was not open in the afternoon because the gods were asleep at that time!

A contrast in understanding the nature of the divine crossed my mind. Unlike the Hindu, but like the Jew, a Christian says, *He who keeps Israel will neither slumber nor sleep. (Psalm 121:4)* The keeper of Israel is the Lord, who made heaven and earth, who keeps believers from all evil, who keeps their life safe, and who keeps their going out and coming in for ever (Psalm 121:2, 7-8). In our prayers and sacred songs we are throwing out a rope to a firm rock, not in order to pull the rock to ourselves, but to pull ourselves to the rock. This rock is God who neither slumbers nor sleeps.

In the New Testament God is known as Father, Son, and Holy Spirit, the One in Three and the Three in One. We know God the Father because we know Jesus the Son and we know that it is through the Son that the Spirit comes and helps us to pray and sing to God.

At the end of our survey of prayers and songs in the New Testament, we think of a prayer which has been turned into a song. The prayer was written by Richard, who was Bishop of Chichester for eight years in mid thirteenth century England.

Thanks be to you, our Lord Jesus Christ,
for all the benefits which you have given us,
for all the pains and insults which you have borne for us.
Most merciful Redeemer, Friend and Brother,
may we know you more clearly,
love you more dearly,
and follow you more nearly,
day by day.
Amen.

This prayer was incorporated by Stephen Schwartz into the song *Day by Day* as part of the 1971 musical Godspell, which was mainly based on the Gospel of Matthew. Jesus was portrayed as a clown who tells parables.

The song *Day by Day* includes the words:

> *Oh Dear Lord*
> *Three things I pray*
> *To see thee more clearly*
> *Love thee more dearly*
> *Follow thee more nearly*
> *Day by day*

Praying and singing belong together. The prayers and songs of the New Testament encourage us to think, to speak, and to act in accord with the God who speaks to us through the Bible.

The inimitable Scot, William Barclay, mentions a brilliant youth who never fulfilled his promise. There were three stages in his career. At one time people said, 'He will do something.' At another time people said, 'He could do something if he would.' Finally, people said, 'He might have done something, if he had liked.' The challenge is for us to pray to the Lord, to sing his praises, to practise what we preach. Otherwise, we may become people who never fulfil our promise.

A Benediction

*Depart now
in the fellowship of God the Father,
and as you go, remember:
in the goodness of God
you were born into this world;
by the grace of God
you have been kept all the day long,
even unto this hour;
and by the love of God,
fully revealed in the face of Jesus,
you are being redeemed. Amen.*

John R. Claypool

Select Bibliography

A Prayer Book for Australia (Broughton Books, 1998)
Barclay, William. *The Daily Study Bible Volumes 1-18*
   (Saint Andrew Press, 1975-1978)
Barrett, C. K. *The Epistle to the Romans* (A & C Black, 1991)
_____ *The Second Epistle to the Corinthians*
   (A & C Black, 1973)
Bauckham, Richard J. *Jude, 2 Peter* (Word Books, 1983)
Beasley-Murray, G. R. *The Book of Revelation*
   (Oliphants, 1974)
Blevins, James L. *Revelation as Drama* (Broadman, 1984)
Boxall, Ian. *The Revelation of Saint John* (A & C Black, 2006)
Brown, Raymond E. *The Birth of the Messiah*
   (Doubleday, 1977)
_____ *The Gospel according to John Vols. 1 & 2*
   (Doubleday, 1966, 1974)
Bruce, F. F. *The Epistle to the Hebrews* (Eerdmans, 1990)
Caird, G. B. *Saint Luke* (Penguin, 1963)
_____ *Paul's Letters from Prison* (Oxford, 1976)
_____ *The Revelation of St John the Divine*
   (A & C Black, 1966)
Campolo, Tony. *Let Me Tell You A Story*
   (W Publishing Group, 2000)
_____ *Stories That Feed Your Soul* (Regal, 2010)
Carey, William. *An Enquiry Into The Obligations Of Christians*
   To Use Means For The Conversion Of The Heathens
   New facsimile edition with an introduction by E. A.
   Payne (Carey Kingsgate Press, 1961)
Chalke, Steve. *The Lost Message of Jesus* (Zondervan, 2003)
Clements, Ronald E. *In Spirit and in Truth: Insights from*
   Biblical Prayers (John Knox, 1985)

Coggan, Donald. *The Prayers of the New Testament* (Hodder & Stoughton, 1967)

Cooke, Alistair. *Six Men* (Penguin Books, 1977)

Craddock, Fred B. 'The Letter to the Hebrews,' *The New Interpreter's Bible*, 12:1-173 (Abingdon, 1998)

Culpepper, R. Alan. *The Gospel and Letters of John* (Fortress, 1998)

_____ 'The Gospel of Luke,' *The New Interpreter's Bible*, 9:1-490 (Abingdon, 1995)

Danker, Frederick William. *A Greek-English Lexicon of the New Testament and other Early Christian Literature* (University of Chicago Press, 2000)

Dodd, C.H. *The Epistle to the Romans* (Collins, 1959)

_____ *The Interpretation of the Fourth Gospel* (Cambridge, 1953)

Dubreuil, Brian. '9/11 and Canada,' *The Canadian Encyclopedia* https://www.thecanadianencyclopedia.ca/en/article/canada-and-911

Fuller, Reginald H. *The Foundations of New Testament Christology* (Scribners, 1965)

Hinson, E. Glenn. *A Serious Call to a Contemplative Lifestyle* (Smyth & Helwys, 1993)

Hooker, Morna. 'The Letter to the Philippians,' *The New Interpreter's Bible*, 11:467-549 (Abingdon, 2000)

Hull, William E. 'John,' *The Broadman Bible Commentary*, 9:189-376 (Broadman, 1970)

Jeremias, Joachim. *The Eucharistic Words of Jesus* (SCM, 1966)

_____ *Jesus and the Message of the New Testament* (Fortress, 2002)

_____ *New Testament Theology Part One The Proclamation of Jesus* (SCM, 1971)

Kelly, J. N. D. *The Epistles of Peter and of Jude*
 (Harper & Row, 1969)
Lincoln, Andrew T. 'The Letter to the Colossians,' *The New Interpreter's Bible*, 11:551-669 (Abingdon, 2000)
Long, Thomas G. *Hebrews* (John Knox Press, 1997)
_____ *Matthew* (Westminster John Knox Press, 1997)
Marshall, I. Howard. *The Gospel of Luke: A Commentary on the Greek Text* (Paternoster, 1978)
Martin, Ralph P. *Carmen Christi: Philippians ii.5-11 in Recent Interpretation and in the Setting of Early Christian Worship* (Cambridge, 1967)
_____ *Colossians: The Church's Lord and the Christian's Liberty* (Paternoster, 1972)
Montefiore, Hugh W. *The Epistle to the Hebrews*
 (A & C Black, 1964)
Moule, C. F. D. *An Idiom-Book of New Testament Greek*
 (Cambridge, 1963)
_____ 'Further Reflexions on Philippians 2:5-11' *Apostolic History and the Gospel [Festschrift for F. F. Bruce]*, pp 264-276. Edited by W. W. Gasque & R. P. Martin (Paternoster, 1970)
Sanders, Jack T. *The New Testament Christological Hymns*
 (Cambridge, 1971)
Stagg, Frank. *New Testament Theology* (Broadman, 1962)
_____ 'Matthew,' *The Broadman Bible Commentary*,
 8:61-253 (Broadman, 1969)
Torbet, Robert G. *A History of the Baptists* (Judson Press, 1973)
Van de Weyer, Robert. Editor. *The Fount Book of Prayer*
 (HarperCollins, 1993)
Williams, Rowan. 'The Lord's Prayer'
 www.bbc.co.uk/religions/christianity/prayer/lordsprayer

Witherington, III, Ben. *John's Wisdom* (John Knox, 1995)
_____ *Incandescence: Light Shed through the Word* (Eerdmans, 2006)
Wright, N. T. *The Climax of the Covenant* (Fortress, 1993)
_____ *The Last Word* (HarperOne, 2005)
_____ 'The Letter to the Romans,' *The New Interpreter's Bible*, 10:393-770 (Abingdon, 2002)
_____ *The Lord and His Prayer* (SPCK, 1996)
_____ *The New Testament for Everyone* (SPCK, 2011)
Yancey, Philip. *Prayer: Does It Make Any Difference?* (Hodder & Stoughton, 2006)
Zerwick, Max. *A Grammatical Analysis of the Greek New Testament Vols. 1 & 2* Translated and revised by Mary Grosvenor (Biblical Institute Press, 1974, 1979)
_____ *Biblical Greek* Translated and revised by Joseph Smith (Biblical Institute Press, 1963)

www.ingramcontent.com/pod-product-compliance
Lightning Source LLC
Chambersburg PA
CBHW030259010526
44107CB00053B/1762